Christia
The Magical Use

Agostino Taumaturgo

Copyright © 2005-2006 and 2015
Agostino Taumaturgo and THAVMA Publications
All rights reserved

Thavma Publications
Columbus, Ohio

Like us on Facebook!
http://facebook.com/OccultCatholicism

TABLE OF CONTENTS

TABLE OF CONTENTS ....- 3 -

FOREWORD AND INTRODUCTION ....- 5 -

I. CANDLES IN CHRISTIANITY..................................- 7 -
   A Christian's Life in Candles ....- 8 -
   At the Votive Rack..- 11 -

II. THE ROLE OF COLOR IN CANDLE MAGIC ......- 13 -
   Biological Reactions to the Visible Spectrum ....- 14 -
   Psychological Reactions to the Visible Spectrum .....- 17 -
   Magical Applications ....- 19 -

III. WORKING WITH THE SAINTS ....- 23 -
   The Praying Church ....- 23 -
   Is This a Catholic Thing?..- 23 -
   The Church Triumphant..- 25 -
   Offerings to the Saints ....- 26 -
   Making Contact with the Saints..................................- 28 -
   A List of Commonly-Invoked Saints.........................- 29 -
   Prayers in Honor of the Saints ....- 51 -

IV. CANDLES, RELICS, MEDALS, TALISMANS...- 53 -
   Candles as a Sacramental..- 53 -
   Types of Candles...- 57 -
   Working with the Candles ....- 61 -
   Relics and Medals...- 65 -
   Talismans (Amulets and Seals)...................................- 67 -

V. MAGIC AND THE ROSARY....................................- 69 -
   Some Magical Uses...- 69 -
   Magical Purposes and the Mysteries..........................- 73 -
   The Proper Use of the Rosary.....................................- 78 -
   Rosary Novenae ....- 79 -

VI. PRACTICAL CANDLE OPERATIONS ....- 80 -
  Love ....- 80 -
  Money ....- 93 -
  Health ....- 103 -
  Protection ....- 108 -

VII. IT'S OVER ALREADY? ....- 110 -
  Reading Your Candles ....- 110 -
  Incense ....- 111 -
  Disposing of Your Materials ....- 112 -
  The End ....- 113 -

APPENDIX A. PRAYERS TO THE SAINTS ....- 114 -
  I. In Honor of Our Lord ....- 114 -
  II. To the Holy Family ....- 116 -
  III. In Honor of Mary ....- 117 -
  IV. In Honor of St. Joseph ....- 119 -
  V. In Honor of the Angels ....- 120 -
  VI. In Honor of the Saints ....- 124 -

APPENDIX B. OILS AND INCENSES ....- 146 -

NOTES ....- 148 -

FOREWORD AND INTRODUCTION

In times present as well as in times past, light has been an ancient fixture of our Christian faith, of our lives, and indeed a necessity of our very existence. If we were to imagine the caveman, for example, when he first saw a lightning bolt strike a tree and create flame, we could just imagine how his eyes and his mind were filled with wonder. For here he was, a lowly creature, a hunted animal himself, vulnerable to predators, to harsh winters, and to any other calamity that nature saw fit to throw at him. But here, in this split instant, the gift of fire gave him power to change all that! The heat scared off his would-be attackers, the cold of the winter could be staved off, and in other ways the quality of his life was surely improved. And thus indeed, for this early man, fire was magical.

As time went on, man learned how to create his own fires, and how to use fire for such things as cooking, boiling water for bathing, and even for weaponry. But there always still remained the wonder of that first man ever to behold the flames, which translated into a mysticism and a magical fascination, and we see that every major religion incorporates fire into its symbolism and practices through one way or another.

"For the Lord our God is a consuming fire."
– Deuteronomy 4:24

As Christians, we ourselves are the heirs to a rich tradition revolving around light and fire, for Jesus called Himself the light and the life of the world, and in those days all light involved some kind of fire (tallow candles, oil lamps, etc.). In the account of Pentecost, we are told that the Holy Ghost came upon the Apostles, which event is commonly depicted in art by each of them having a tongue of fire over their heads. And in the liturgical (ritual-oriented) churches, fire still plays an integral part through the use of candles and incense, both of which often call to mind memories of special, happier, and more reverent times when we were young, and speak of a majesty and a glory connected with the service of the Sacred.

But there have been other uses of these lights as well, besides those which has been afforded by religion. Amongst Catholic populations in Mediterranean and Latin American countries, and in other areas around the world where Christianity has spread, there are folk traditions such as Curanderismo and Benedicaria which incorporate candle burning techniques and incense into their magical and spiritual practices, and yet again the fire is a thing of fixation, one's desire being manifested while the candle burns and the Saints are being invoked.

And so it is that we set forth with this book, in which we shall explore the uses of candles that are all around us as citizens of the New Jerusalem, from their use in formal religious observances to the folk magical traditions that exist amongst Christian populations in Europe and America, and from there we shall endeavor to demonstrate that candle-burning magic can be worked in such a way as to be perfectly proper for a devout and practicing Christian of even the most Conservative or Traditionalist stripe.

I. CANDLES IN CHRISTIANITY

As we begin, we find ourselves coming full circle to the one place where many of our readers may have been born, or may have left, or to which have come as their new spiritual home, or perhaps even fled only to return later: the faith delivered by Jesus to the Apostles.

According to the Right Reverend John F. Sullivan, in his *The Visible Church* (1920, P.J. Kennedy & Sons, New York), the use of candles in worship predates Christianity, and he goes on to give examples of how Jews and Pagans also used candles in their worship. We ourselves could go on to say that they were also used by Hindus, Buddhists, and just about every other religion whose adherents had the technology to make them.

Now before our more scrupulous readers become mortified by any association with Paganism, and before any Fundamentalist readers can start jumping up and down with that "See! This whole book is Pagan and therefore of SATAN!!!" crap that they like to run off at the mouth about, let me nip this thing in the bud right now.

An object, such as a candle, or a bead, or a vestment, or a head-covering, or an altar, or a symbol, or whatever, is simply an inanimate object and in no way ties to a specific religion. In fact, such things as these are universal to all religions and find themselves used in different ways. For example, a bead can be used to make a necklace, or it can be used to make a string of Buddhist prayer beads, or it can be used to make a Catholic Rosary, and so on and so forth. The same can be said of candles, which can be used to mark the Four Quarters in Neopagan and Neohermetic rites, or they can be used as an offering made to deity, or a secular dignitary (as was done in late Roman times), or to the One true God. The object is neutral, while its good or evil usage is determined by the person who uses it.

A Christian's Life in Candles
Traditionally, candles play an integral part in the historic rites of Christian worship, and in liturgical churches, they are used in the administration of all the Sacraments with the exception of Penance. With this in mind, let's take a brief journey through a typical "high-church" ritual and sacramental life, and demonstrate how illumined it is by the light of a candle.

Before we begin, I should point out that this tour applies to the more "high church" and "magisterial" churches. If your background is more "broad church," "low church," or derived from the Radical Reformation, your mileage may vary greatly. In fact, the more "high-church" you are by nature, the more likely you'll have an intuitive grasp of some of the principles given in this book.

Moving on . . .

At the first stage of a newborn Christian's life, he is taken to be baptized. Since we all know the details of this ceremony and the grace conferred by this sacrament, it is noteworthy to mention something that occurs at the end of the ceremony in some churches. At this point, the priest or minister gives a lighted candle to the newly baptized, and the *Rituale Romanum* (the Catholic Church's book of rituals before the late 60's) tells the priest to say:

"Receive this burning light, and keep thy Baptism so as to be without blame: keep the commandments of God, that when the Lord shall come to the wedding-feast, thou mayest meet Him together with all the Saints in the heavenly court, and mayest thou have eternal life and live forever. Amen."

In this ceremony, the candle is a symbol of the purity of Sanctifying Grace which the newly-baptized person has received through this sacrament. It's an expression not only of the wondrous gift God has just given him, but also of an (ideally) ardent desire to keep that gift unblemished throughout his entire life.

This is probably the most dramatic use the Church has for a candle in a one-on-one context, although as a high-church Christian goes through life, he will particularly notice the candles at Mass (the Lord's Supper) and also at the votive candle racks along the side-walls of some churches.

At the Service itself, the Church uses candles to represent the light of Christ shining in the world, and this symbolism is especially brought out in the "Sanctuary Light," a red candle or oil lamp that some churches keep perpetually lit. The red of this light represents the blood of Christ poured out for all humanity, and this light serves both to announce His presence to us, as well as remind us of that Sacrifice which He made for us on the Cross.

Of the general symbolism of candles, I will quote Sullivan again, when he says:

"Light is pure; it penetrates darkness; it moves with incredible velocity; it nourishes life; it illumines all around it. Therefore it is a symbol of God, the All-Pure, existing everywhere, giving life and enlightenment. It also represents our Blessed Saviour and His mission, for He is 'the Light of the World,' to enlighten 'them that sit in darkness and in the shadow of death.'

"In the candle, the wax, being spotless, represents Christ's spotless Body. The wick enclosed in the wax is an image of

His Soul; and the candle-flame typifies the Divine Nature united to the human in one Divine Person."
(*The Visible Church*, p. 159)

In liturgical churches, this symbolism is brought to its grandest display on Holy Saturday night, and continuing all the way until the Feast of the Ascension forty days later, where we find a custom of lighting the Paschal Candle. This candle is large (over three feet long and two inches thick in many cases), and blessed during the Easter Vigil. It's then used in the blessing of the baptismal font – where we see the candle's bottom part immersed thrice in a fertility-rite type of gesture – and five grains of incense are inserted into its side as a sign of the Five Wounds of Our Savior. The candle is then placed on a stand to the left-hand side of the altar and lit at all services during the forty days after Easter Sunday, finally to be extinguished during the Service on Ascension Thursday. The Paschal Candle is seen as a symbol of the Risen Christ, and His presence amongst us for those forty days before He ascended into Heaven.

Still keeping in line with our current discussion, we have thus far discussed the use of candles in baptism and the Communion Service. Throughout the administration of the other sacraments candles are used, but they're generally in the background with a purpose of expressing Christ's presence in the ritual about to be celebrated. That said, in some of the more liturgically-oriented churches there's a common practice of placing a candle in a dying man's hand, so that at both the beginning and the end of his Christian life he is accompanied by the light of those graces which he has received, and the promise of eternal glory that awaits him should he have lived faithfully in accordance with the teachings of Our Lord.

At the Votive Rack

In the previous section, I made reference to the votive candle stands found along the side walls of some church buildings. They're commonly found in front of a statue of some or other Saint, and the candles themselves are combinations of small votive candles and large seven-day lights, next to a sign with suggested donations for each candle. Having been in ministry, I can say from experience that the donation actually is the cost of the candle itself, so rest assured that the sign is no attempt to get rich off the parishioners. Rather, it's a plea to help cover the cost of what you're using!

In the life of the average lay Christian, this votive stand is the place where candle burning practices come closest to being united with Christian piety. In common practice, either before or after Services the faithful will either a) light one candle for the living and one for the dead, or b) light one or more candles for their personal intentions. The light itself is an offering to God that your prayers may be heard, while the smoke of the candle, much like the smoke of incense, is a sign of your prayers being offered to God. One could also say that the flame of the candle is your petition to the heavens carried upwards by the smoke. The color of the candle is the symbolic expression of your intention (we'll discuss this later), and the spotless wax is the purity of your intention as you lay yourself bare before God the Father. In this sense, the candle becomes you and represents you offering yourself to God in exchange for the fulfillment of your prayer, being consumed by God as the candle is consumed by the flame.

Yet this votive rack is more than just a place from which you offer your prayers to the Creator and ask the Saints to intercede on your behalf. Ultimately this rack, this shelf, is the source and focal point from which all Candle Magic flows, and to which it all returns. The folk traditions of rural peasants (i.e. Benedicaria, Curanderismo, Hoodoo, etc.) all burn candles as offerings to God and to the Saints in exchange for their activity on the petitioner's behalf, and the color scheme is almost universally the same. They may use roots, they may use herbs, they may even incorporate specific folk or magical lore which comes from each country's indigenous or even pre-Christian traditions, but the processes of modern candle-burning techniques and the colors associated with them all find their common beginnings on that votive candle rack, most commonly found next to the side altar of Joseph and/or Mary at your local Catholic or High Anglican Church.

II. THE ROLE OF COLOR IN CANDLE MAGIC

Ever since time immemorial, man has looked around and marveled at the world and the many colors with which it is painted. Hues of brilliant reds, peaceful blues, wondrous greens, delightful orange, rich saffron, somber black and brilliant white. In his common parlance, he would speak of color to communicate thoughts or feelings ("red with rage" or "green with envy," for example), and as he looked to the heavens he would paint the orbs contained therein with layers of symbol and color. In his ceremonies, he would employ different implements and robes of various shades and hues, and would associate different colors with different levels of spiritual realms in his mystical exercises.

Now understand, dear reader, that these things did not take place overnight, but rather were the result of countless thousands of years of custom, evolution, development, and experimentation. The time span running from the primordial muck of mankind's beginnings to even the Sumerian and Egyptian civilizations measured countless millennia at least, and over those millennia did early man's consciousness evolve and his awareness of the other-than-physical realms deepen, to such a point that he could work out a system of rituals and symbols to contact the denizens of those realms.

As he looked around and developed these systems of rituals which abounded in the ancient world, he always noted the color of what was around him. He noted the rich green of fertile plant life, the browns of the earth, the red hues of fire and of blood that poured out from his enemies' flesh, the black of night and of dried blood (again from his slain enemies), the blue of a sky at high noon, the yellow of the sun and of gold, the silvery-white of clouds or the moon, and so on and so on.

Biological Reactions to the Visible Spectrum
Over the course of time, these observations evolved and color became symbolic not only of the world around him and the spiritual realms which surround and penetrate this one, but likewise of the world inside humankind. Color represented his emotions, his diseases, his strengths, and his weaknesses, and so forth. Following this logic, many color- healers would either construct or learn systems of healing by color, which was especially popular from the late nineteenth century to the New Age movement of today.

One school of these researchers or healers, in which we could include **George Starr White** (*The Story of the Human Aura*, 1928), **Walter J. Kilner** (*The Human Atmosphere*, 1911), and **Oscar Bagnale** (*The Origin and Properties of the Human Aura*, 1937), based their observations and/or cures on observing a person's aura, noting its strengths and deficiencies, what conditions it may indicate, and then prescribing lights, clothing, or visualizations of some appropriate color to heal or otherwise change the condition in question.

Another school of these researchers or healers, who can be called "chromopaths" such as **S. Pancoast** (*Red and Blue Light*, 1877) and **Edwin Babbit** (*The Principles of Light and Color*, 1896), who would diagnose the ailment in some or other fashion, and then prescribe cures based on color. Generally speaking, red would be prescribed for paralysis or exhaustion, yellow and orange to stimulate the nerves, blue and violet to soothe inflammatory or nervous conditions, and many combinations of these could be effected.

I mention these authors because it's not just the interior designer who pays attention to how color affects the body and mind, and should we pay attention to these effects, the better to harness them in our candle burning or any other type of magic. In this, it must be considered that color is a part of the electromagnetic spectrum, albeit a very small part at that. As Faber Birren said in the classic work on the subject, *Color Psychology and Color Therapy* (1961, Citadel Press, Seacaucus, NJ.), *"All electromagnetic energy – including visible color – will effect the human organism."* Ultraviolet rays tan the skin, X-rays penetrate the body, and Infrared rays can keep our food warm; the visible spectrum is likewise a part of that electromagnetic energy. In fact, Birren's text will be the basis for what I have to say about this subject.

Before we go further, let's take a moment to consider that what we call "color" is in fact nothing more than reflected light. When a ray of white light (containing all colors) shines on a red surface, for example, it absorbs all other colors and reflects back only the red area of the visible spectrum. Our eyes notice this red light being reflected back, and we interpret this as "seeing a red object." Thus it's the reflection of red light that enables us to see the color red; the same holds true for blue, green, or any other color.

In 1900, Oscar Raab experimented with dyes and their toxicity. He found that when undyed organisms were exposed to light, they could survive for long periods of time. However, when he dyed the organisms, they became sensitive to light (i.e. absorbed the part of the visible spectrum which the dye didn't reflect), and they died.

As a result of Raab's research, the physiological effects of color on humans became a subject for more experimentation. In 1940 the Japanese doctors Natume and

Mizutani found, for example, that blue dyes (which absorb red light) quickened the healing of wounds, while red dye (which absorbed blue but reflected red light) served to retard it. These results were published along with the findings of Dr. Kotaro Menju, who found that milk secretion was accelerated in pigs irradiated with red light, while it was retarded in those irradiated with blue light. ("Effect of Visible Light upon the Secretion of Milk," *Japanese Journal of Obstetrics and Gynecology*. June, 1940.)

To me, these results seem amazingly similar to Pancoast's claims about red and blue light, although these experiments took place in more controlled conditions and thus come across as more credible.

According to Birren, in 1910 a man named Stein experimented with colored light and the ability of the muscles to respond (called tonus), and then goes on to mention the work of A. Metzger, whose experiment had his subjects stretch their arms horizontally in front of their bodies. Red light would cause the arms to spread away from each other, while green light would cause them to approach each other in a series of jerky motions. (Birren, pp. 130-131).

What do we learn from these experiments? We learn that the spectrum of visible light has an effect on us. The red/orange range stimulates us, while the violet/blue range relaxes us and even has slight germicidal properties. The middle or yellow/green region of the spectrum, however, seems to be pretty neutral when it comes to affecting one's physiology.

Psychological Reactions to the Visible Spectrum
When we enter the realm of psychology and the mind's reaction to the visible spectrum's radiation, we enter a different realm entirely. Although little attention is often paid to the use of color in American medicine, psychological studies on the subject are more common.

Before going forward, I'd like to point out that most experimentation with color is carried out with lights instead of painted objects. The reason for this is that the eye of the subject is saturated with the color in question, which then makes the effect more pronounced. I plan to revisit this subject later, when we get into the subject of candle burning and actual magical practice.

In the first place, mankind has always has an emotional response to color. Whether he loves a particular color or hates it, or if a certain shade may disgust him (how many times do we say *"That color makes me want to vomit?"*), there's a definite emotional response to color in human beings.

In tests which are used to determine personality type, such as Roschach or Luscher, a person's response to various colors is used to determine aspects of that person's character, which gives us a clue as to how deeply color really affects us.

This is that interests us, the manner in which color influences the mind in and of itself, as well as how it influences the body through means of the mind. In the research of Kuer Goldstein, we read of a woman with a cerebellar disease who tended to walk unsteadily and fall unexpectedly. When she wore a red dress, this tendency increased, and when she wore a blue or green dress, her equilibrium was almost normal. (Goldstein, Kurt. "Some

Experimental Observations Concerning the Influence of Color on the Function of the Organism," *Occupational Therapy and Rehabilitation*. June, 1942.)

Goldstein also speaks of people with tremors and who tend to twitch, and tells us that they may alleviate these symptoms by wearing green glasses. His reason is that the glasses filter out red light.

If we take anything away from all this, we can glean that the red end of the spectrum has the potential to disrupt, confuse, and stimulate, while the blue end has potential to relax and silence. The green middle can signify withdrawal into oneself and return to the quiet center.

Interestingly enough, this reminds me of *The Wizard of Oz* – the book, not the movie – where the inhabitants of Emerald City were compelled to paint everything green, wear only green clothes, and wear green glasses, because the Wizard's favorite color was green. Could it be that the Wizard, who left Kansas and crossed the desert surrounding this mystical land, could no longer handle the outer world and wanted to remain withdrawn into his own quiet center? I'll let the reader decide.

Also interesting to note is that perception of time and measurement can differ under varying colors of light. As Birren notes (quoting Goldstein), people tend to overestimate time under red light and underestimate it under blue or green light. He also says that under red light, people overestimate the measurement of objects (e.g. the length of a stick) and underestimate them in blue or green light. The same goes for weight estimations as well. Warm colors cause things to seem bigger, and cool colors cause them to seem smaller. (Birren, p. 146)

Many experiments have also been conducted regarding the relation of color with music, odors, and food, and our everyday slang also resonates with the psychological aspects of color. The really cool thing about all this research and experimentation is that it shows the human fascination with color is not just a figment of the imagination or a flight of fancy; it's a hard scientific fact around which we find many mysteries and much symbolism, and through which we can apply color to accomplish our designs.

Magical Applications
Since the dawn of time, magicians have been quick to pick up on and utilize color and color symbolism in their magical systems. Seeing that color, like sound, is a simple thing to absorb and appreciate, and how color surrounds and permeates every part of our lives and our being, it becomes an easy leap to see how magicians and religionists the world over would incorporate it into their work.

The use of color in the Church has been covered in detail in the many prayer books and hand-missals which have been published over the past century, and the magical uses of the Church's colors have been discussed thoroughly in my *The Magic of Catholicism* (2015. THAVMA Publications). These colors are similar to, and perhaps the root source of, the symbolism and use of the colors traditionally employed by candle magicians of virtually every stripe. The colors of the visible spectrum are also attributed to the seven planets known to ceremonial magicians, the seven notes of the musical scale, and the seven chakras found in eastern mystical systems.

In his book, *Practical Color Magick* (1983, Llewellyn Publications), Neopagan author Raymond Buckland discusses techniques to incorporate color into one's magical practices, some of which I find rather interesting. The first is what he calls "CM," or "Color Meditation," consisting of meditation while wearing a robe with circles or bands of color covering the seven eastern chakras, while imagining light of the corresponding color shining into these centers. This is followed by a number of exercises relating color to psychic development, and then a system of rituals which invoke no entities but simply use colored candles and cloth pockets, combined with the imposition of the operator's will onto the subject.

The systems of various magical orders associate color with the vestments and robes used in their organization's rituals, or in the private rituals of its practitioners. This is akin to the "color of the day" used not only in the Catholic Church and in Protestant churches which follow the pattern of the Church year: Lutherans, Anglicans, Methodists, United Church of Christ, and countless others.

In the Hermetic Order or Golden Dawn, there was a technique called a "flashing tablet," where a sigil or talisman was made of complimentary colors, so as better to attract the "Akashic Light." (Israel Regardie, *The Golden Dawn*, 1995 [Sixth Edition], Llewellyn Publications. pp. 481-504: "Talismans and Sigils.")

As a general rule of thumb, the use of color in magic deals with coloring anything from candles, ink, paper, clothing, and even the walls of a room, with each color being applied to a specific purpose:

1. Red is commonly utilized for works involving passionate love, blood, strength, vigor, or energy. It is associated with the planet Mars and C on the musical scale. In the Church it is the color of blood and the color of charity, worn on

feasts of the Martyrs, of the Holy Cross, and the Holy Ghost.

2. Orange is commonly utilized in rites of healing, stimulation, or encouragement. It is associated with the planet Mercury and D on the musical scale.

3. Yellow is commonly utilized for works involving joy, happiness, and confidence. It is associated with the Sun and E on the musical scale. Though no longer a vestment color, in the medieval Church this was the color of joy, worn on the feastdays of Confessors.

4. Green is commonly utilized in rites involving hope, fertility, money, and growth. It is associated with the planet Venus and F on the musical scale. In the Church it is the color of growth, hope, and increase, worn during "Ordinary Time," the period after Epiphany and after Pentecost.

5. Blue is commonly used in rites involving peace, devotion, meditation, protection, calming, and tranquility. It is associated with the planet Jupiter and G on the musical scale. Though no longer a vestment color, in the Church this is the color of the Blessed Virgin Mary.

6. Indigo (interchangeable with black) is commonly used in rites involving tension, binding, depression, and death, release, and absorption of negative energy. It is associated with the planet Saturn and A on the musical scale. As black, in the Church this is the color of death; in former times black was worn on Good Friday, the Feast of All Souls (November 2), and at all funerals and Masses for the dead.

7. Violet is commonly used in rites of change, spiritual power, the astral plane, as well as mourning. It is associated

with the Moon and B on the musical scale. In the Church it is the color of mourning and of penance, worn during Advent and Lent. In former times, violet was also worn on Ember Days and during the Rogations.

8. White is commonly used in rites involving purity, innocence, protection, and divine intervention. In the Church it is the color of purity and innocence, worn on all feasts of Our Lord and of the Blessed Virgin Mary, and of saints who are not martyrs.

In the next chapter, we will find that not only do we have this general allocation of color attribution, but that each saint also has his or her own special color, which will figure in as being very important to any Christian pursuing a system of magic with colors and candles.

III. WORKING WITH THE SAINTS

The Praying Church
The idea that man has spiritual helpers is an old one, as old as religion itself. As animism evolved into religion, man began to believe that his ancestors' spirits looked down from their current abode, and could be asked to help their posterity.

In Christianity, this belief lives on in the veneration of the Saints. The Saints, our ancestors in faith, are said to look upon us from heaven and pray for us here below.

Is This a Catholic Thing?
In the western world, the intercession of the Saints is considered a "Catholic" thing, when such is actually far from the truth. The veneration of the Saints is found in the Early Church, from before the split into Western Catholicism and Eastern Orthodoxy, and continues in both churches today.

So why is the intercession of Saints considered "just a Catholic thing?" The short answer lies in the Protestant Reformation. The longer answer lies in the Protestant conception of *worship*.

Reformation-era Protestantism can be said to consist of four distinct factions: Evangelical (Luther), Reformed (Zwingli and Calvin), Anglican (Cranmer), and Anabaptist (Karldstadt, Simonis, et al.). Even though these factions taught conflicting doctrines and were often at each others' throats, they were agreed on five principles called *solas*. These five *solas* were:

1. Sola Scriptura (Scripture Alone)
2. Sola Fide (Faith Alone)

3. Sola Gratia (Grace Alone)
4. Solus Christus (Christ Alone)
5. Soli Deo Gloria (Glory to God Alone)

It's the fourth and fifth *solas*, "Christ Alone" and "Glory to God Alone," that the Protestants took as forbidding honor to the Saints, because Christ was to be seen as our only mediator (1 Timothy 2:5), and veneration of a Saint was construed as giving glory to someone other than God.

Of course, not all Protestants took the hard line. In the *Defense of the Augsburg Confession*, for example, the Lutherans concede that Angels help humanity, and that the Saints constantly pray for us (Article XXI).

Luther himself even said it's okay to pray the first two thirds of the *Hail Mary* (the part that's a quotation of Luke 1:28 and 1:42). It was the Reformed and the Anabaptists who gave the staunchest opposition. Remember that the Reformation was an intellectual and emotional powder keg that left tensions heated for centuries.

Yet those tensions are cooling with the passage of time, and the "mainline" Protestant churches have eased up on their opposition. There seems to be a realization that asking someone for a favor is not the same as worship, and the modern Episcopalian *Book of Common Prayer* even mentions the intercession of Saints specifically in its rite of Christian burial.

In short, no Christian group questioned the intercession of the Saints prior to the Protestant Reformation, and it would seem that the past hundred years of ecumenical scholarship are bringing a more positive reappraisal of the practices of the ancient Church.

The Church Triumphant

Ten years ago, on the now-defunct *Stregoneria Italiana* forums, I had a conversation with an Anglican member who asked whether it's okay to burn a candle for one's ancestors. My response was to give an explanation of the Communion of Saints, the relationship between the Church Triumphant in heaven and the Church Militant on earth. Since we're discussing how the invocation of the Saints pertains to candle burning procedures, I suppose giving some background might be a good idea.

In the first place, it helps to remember the Church Triumphant consists of all the Angels, Saints, Blesseds, and everybody else in heaven, and not just those named in the *Catalogue of Saints* belonging to any church. This can include our ancestors and loved ones, and many others the Church doesn't know about. They watch over and intercede for us, and since they see and know the Big Guy on a personal basis, they know more about him, his rules, and the way he thinks than the rest of us presently do. They could be said to use this special knowledge and act as our lawyers in God's courtroom, helping us to get the favors we ask for and/or need.

This brings us to the Church Militant, and that would be you and me. Actually, the Church Militant consists of all baptized persons still living, fighting the good fight against the temptations and adversities. Of course we don't always fight the good fight, but that's another story.

We receive the help from the legal department in the Church Triumphant, and we also offer them thanks and spread word of their deeds to keep their memory alive here on earth.

At this point, Catholic readers may ask about the "Church Suffering." Since this is meant to be an ecumenical book, I've deliberately chosen not to address this, but at the same time it can't hurt to mention the Catholic belief that the Church Suffering consists of the *poor souls* in Purgatory who can be helped by our good works and prayers, and whom some theologians claim are able to pray and intercede for us, too. I discuss this more in Chapter 6 of my *The Magic of Catholicism*.

Offerings to the Saints
In the folk Catholicism of some countries, there is a custom of offering of food, wine, herbs, or flowers to the Saints. Saint Michael is garlic, St. Joseph is the lily, St. Therese is the rose, St. Jude is mint, and so on.

As I sit writing this chapter, I have on my lap a manuscript copy of Vito Quattrocchi's *The Sicilian Blade II*. In this book Quattrocchi discusses his initiation into the Art of *San Michele*, and he describes his training in Benedicaria. On pages 61 and 62 of the manuscript, he describes being taught by a Benedetta named Santucch, who explained the herbs to him as follows:

"So you're saying that Saint Michael likes garlic?"

"No, San Michele is garlic." She said emphatically.

"Is garlic?" I said incredulously. "How in the world is Saint Michael garlic?" .....

"Si, si, he embodies it, with his essence, his power. Therefore, when you use it for spiritual purposes it becomes him. You will see, you will feel it. All these herbs," she made a sweeping movement with her hand, *"have power; a Saint embodies each of these herbs ... The Saints*

are all around us, everywhere we walk. We just have to know who and where they are. When we need protection, money, or anything we have access to our heavenly helpers."

Later in the manuscript, Vito asks Santucch why food is offered to the Saints, and she answers, "... as we speak to them and develop a relationship with them, they become our friends and as we ask favors of them, they ask favors of us. Over the centuries, we have found out what certain Saints enjoy, and what works when we petition them. That is why we give certain foods to certain Saints." (*The Sicilian Blade II: The Teachings of Don Giuseppe Quattrocchi.* 2005. Self-Published at Lulu.com)

I feel there can be no better explanation than that, in regard to indentifying certain Saints with certain herbs, and the offering of various foods to the Saints. Though many people think the intercession of Saints is a contract relationship where they ask the saint to give them stuff but give nothing in return. And then, when their request fails to fall right into their lap, they automatically assume it's the Saint's fault! Think about it: would you go to a complete stranger and expect them to give you a new car for free?

For that reason, we should look to the Saints as our friends, and become friends with them first and foremost. Sit, meditate, light a candle, and say "Hi" to the Saint for no particular reason, just to get acquainted. Sit, meditate, have a friendly conversation in your mind with him or her. But whatever you do, don't start asking for things unless it's a definite emergency! Just get acquainted first, and know that it's from your friendship that good things start to flow.

For starters, I'd recommend beginning with your patron Saint, then maybe branching out to the Saints to whom you feel most drawn. Maybe a simple exercise like the one below:

Making Contact with the Saints

1. On your mensa or home altar, place a holy card or a statue of the Saint of your choice in the center. Either before or to the side of the image, place a candle of the Saint's color on the mensa, and you may also have a plate with food or with herbs proper to the Saint.

2. Cross yourself in the usual manner, and light the candle, saying: **I offer this candle and this food (or this herb) to Saint N., that we may come to know each other in friendship and in co-operation. Saint N., may we become fast friends, that I may follow your example here on earth, and in heaven may you intercede on my behalf before the throne of the Almighty Father.**

3. Sit comfortably in a chair and relax, using whatever relaxative/meditative procedure you desire. After that, mentally greet the Saint in your own words, or pray a chaplet to that Saint (if he or she has one), or some other suitable devotion.

4. After as long a time as feels appropriate (usually 10-20 minutes), feel free to close the meditation. **Saint N., I have enjoyed our time together. May almighty God richly bless you, and may we again meet soon.**

5. Cross yourself in the usual manner, completing the exercise.

Through this exercise, we can become closer with the Saints by talking to them as friends, inviting them into our lives to help us, and offering our help to them. This can be considered a hallmark of Christian piety, and definitely a practical application of the doctrine of the Communion of Saints.

A List of Commonly-Invoked Saints

Below is a list of some of commonly-invoked saints and the areas of life they cover. This is a "starter list" to acquaint the reader with who does what, and a great wealth of additional information may be available on the internet.

1 - Agnes
St. Agnes was a Roman virgin who suffered martyrdom at the age of thirteen, rather than lose her virginity.
Feast: January 21
Candle Color: Blue or White
Symbol: Lamb
Invoke to keep a husband faithful, find a soul mate, or reveal dishonesty in a relationship (find out the truth about someone).

2 - Alexis
The legend of St. Alexis, the "Man of God," tells us that he abandoned wealth and power and lived in poverty and anonymity until his identity was revealed after his death.
Feast: July 17
Candle Color: Pink
Symbol: Crucifix
Invoke to ask for protection from astral attack, violence and enemies.

3 - Alphonsus Liguori
St. Alphonsus is renowned as a great moral theologian and for his works of devotion, and founder of the Redemptorist Order.
Feast: August 2
Candle Color: Purple

Invoke to ask for help with muscle aches, joint pain and arthritis, or for anything to do with the bones. He is also the patron Saint of moral theologians and responsible for our present-day prayers on the Way of the Cross.

4 - Aloysius
From his infancy St. Aloysius displayed extraordinary purity and devotion to our Blessed Lady. At the age of 17 he entered the Society of Jesus in which he distinguished himself for his detachment from the world, faithfulness to rule, and warm charity towards his brethren. He is the patron of Catholic youth.
Feast: June 21
Candle Color: Blue
Invoke to settle domestic disputes and also banish flu, fevers and contagious diseases.

5 - Anne, Mother of the Virgin Mary
We have no historical knowledge of St. Anne, but her praises are sung by many Fathers of the early Church. Christians in all ages have had a tender devotion to her, and she is the patroness of Christian mothers.
Feast: July 26
Candle Color: White
She is the patron Saint of grandmothers, housekeepers, housewives, mothers and women in labor. Petition her for help with the deaf and the blind, and may also be petitioned to help with creating a peaceful and happy home environment.

6 - Anthony of Padua
St. Anthony, a Franciscan, was famed for his learning and for his wonderful success as a preacher. God worked innumerable miracles through St. Anthony, his fame as a wonderworker has led him be venerated worldwide,

especially in the form of contributing to "St. Anthony's Bread" for the poor.
Feast: June 13
Candle Color: Brown
Symbol: Lily
To Invoke: burn a brown candle for special requests, a green candle for financial help or an orange candle to find a husband. St. Anthony's is a wonderworker when it comes to finding lost articles, improving the memory and bringing back a strayed lover.

7 - Augustine of Hippo
Aurelius Augustinus was born in northern Africa to a pagan father and a Catholic mother (St. Monica). After many years of philosophical searching, he was finally converted by the prayers of his mother and baptized by St. Ambrose of Milan. His thinking influenced not only the course of Church teaching, but also the whole of Western philosophy and political thinking till the sixteenth century. He is considered the greatest of the Early Fathers, and alongside Aquinas is the foremost Doctor of the Church. Because of his former loose living he is the patron Saint of brewers.
Feast: August 28
Candle Color: White
Invoke to gain the gift of eloquence in rhetoric or philosophy, or to brew a perfect batch of beer.

8 - Barbara
St. Barbara was a native of Asia Minor. After long imprisonment and torture because of her faith, she was beheaded in Nicomedia.
Feast: December 4
Candle Color: Red
Symbol: Tower
Invoke to protect your relationship from rivals, to protect yourself from meddling in-laws, to clear your path of

obstacles, to help someone be released from prison and for protection from storms. She is also the patroness of wives whose men are at war.

9 - Bartholomew the Apostle
After the Ascension of Our Lord and the coming of the Holy Ghost, St. Bartholomew preached the Gospel in the East. A constant tradition tells that he was beaten to death in Armenia where he had converted large numbers to the faith, including the sister of the king.
Feast: August 24
Candle Color: Red
Symbol: Butcher Knife
Invoke to reveal the truth to you if you feel like something is being hidden or concealed from you. You can also ask him for protection from violence, violent death and protection and healing while undergoing surgery.

10 - Benedict
St. Benedict, the founder of Western monasticism and of the Benedictine Order. His order gave innumerable Saints to the Church, and was instrumental in propagating the faith through the barbarian nations of Europe and the great civilizing force in the early Middle Ages.
Feast: March 21
Candle Color: White
Symbol: Raven, Broken Cup
Invoke to ask for protection against a variety of evil influences: against poisons, evil temptations, contagious diseases, safety during storms, and assistance during times of healing and death. Saint Benedict also helps heal animals and increase prosperity.

11 - Blaise
St. Blaise was bishop of Sebaste in Armenia in the fourth century. In his lifetime he was famed for many miracles,

including the healing of sick animals. He suffered death by beheading for the faith. To this day, the Catholic Church has a blessing of throats seeking his intercession every year on his feast-day.
Feast: February 3
Candle Color: Blue
Symbol: Comb, Two Unlit Crossed Candles
Invoke to increase positive communication and self-expression. He also helps with diseases of the throat.

12 - Brigid of Kildare
St. Brigid founded the first convent for women in Ireland, and her life was remarkable for its intense love of Jesus and the Virgin Mary, and for her charity towards the poor. Many miracles showed the power of her intercession with God, and she exercised a great influence for good throughout Ireland, of whom she is regarded as the second patron.
Feast: February 1
Candle Color: Yellow
Symbol: Cow.
Invoke to become fertile, for healing, for happiness and health of pets and farmyard animals, to assist with breeding livestock, for inspiration, for literary gifts (especially poetry) and the gift of prophecy.

13 - Catherine of Alexandria
St. Catherine lived in Alexandra, and during her trial she confuted pagan philosophers who were brought to dispute with her. After various torments, she suffered death by beheading.
Feast: November 25
Candle Color: Yellow or White
Symbol: Wheel

Invoke to petition her for beauty, fertility, a peaceful death, confidence, seductiveness and confidence when public speaking.

14 - Cecilia
Cecilia was a Roman maiden who made a vow of virginity. When given in marriage to a pagan Valerianus, she converted him and his brother Tiburtius to the faith. All three were martyred in the third century, and today St. Cecilia is considered the patron saint of musicians.
Feast: November 22
Candle Color: Green
Symbol: Organ
Invoke for success in a career in the arts, particularly if you are a musician, poet or singer.

15 - Christopher
St. Christopher, whose original name was Reprobus, was a giant who suffered martyrdom under the Emperor Decius, and from the earliest times devotion to him was widespread in the Eastern Church. He received the name Christopher ("Bearer of Christ") from an incident in which he unknowingly carried the infant Jesus on his back across a stream. Devotion to him remains widespread to this very day.
Feast: July 25
Candle Color: Red
Invoke for protection from accidents, sudden death, and against storms. Christopher protects motorists and travelers so he is the one to pray to for a safe journey.

16 - Clare of Assisi
St. Claire is the founder of the Second Order of St. Francis. Her love of God revealed itself in an intense devotion to the Blessed Sacrament.
Feast: August 12

Devotional Color: White
Symbol: Monstrance
Invoke for protection against astral attack and for help overcoming addiction to drugs and alcohol.

17 - Cosmas and Damian

Cosmas and Damian were two Christian physicians who accepted no money for their services. They were imprisoned by the governor Cilicia and beheaded for their refusal to renounce their Faith. Ss. Cosmas and Damian are, with St. Luke, the patrons of medical doctors.
Feast: September 27
Candle Color: Green
Symbol: Herbs and Palm
Invoke for help with doctors and health, to get a correct diagnosis and for general physical protection. He can also clear obstacles from your path.

18 - Cyprian of Antioch

Cyprian of Antioch was born in the third century to a pagan family, and showed a great potential for the magic arts. He trained under the great masters, and was famed for his magic skill and power. Upon his inability to seduce St. Justina by magic spell, Cyprian immediately became a Christian, and was martyred along with St. Justina in the Diocletian persecution of 304.
Feast: September 26
Candle Color: Red or Purple
Invoke to be protected against black magic, conversion attempts by Satanists, to grow in strength as a magician.

19 - Cyprian of Carthage

St. Cyprian of Carthage is one of the Church Fathers of the third century, and is best known for his conception of Church unity. He was exile from Carthage for his faith, and upon returning he was executed for refusing to

sacrifice to idols. Today he is considered the patron of lawyers and orators.
Feast: September 16
Candle Color: Purple
Invoke to be protected from womanizers, liars, cheaters, and negative attitudes. He helps homeless people and those who have been convicted from getting a heavy sentence.

20 - Dymphna
Saint Dymphna was born to a nobleman who, stricken with mental infirmity, searched to no avail for a woman to replace his departed wife. When no woman would marry him, he then decided to turn his affections on his daughter, who received the grace of martyrdom while defending her virginity from his advances in the year 620.
Feast: May 15
Candle Color: Blue
Symbol: Downward-pointing Sword
Invoke for help with nervous disorders, mental afflictions, epilepsy, insanity, obsession and spiritual attack.

21 - Expedite
The name Expeditus is found among a group of martyrs, thought to be either in Rome or from Armenia.
Feast: none
Candle Color: Yellow
Symbol: Cross with the Word *hodie* ("today"), Raven
Invoke to settle disputes or to reverse a negative situation around. This is who you petition to if you need things to change quickly or suddenly.

22 - Florian
St. Florian was an officer in the Roman Army, executed during the persecution of Diocletian. His intercession is attributed to many cases of healing and protection from fire and flooding.

Feast: May 4
Candle Color: Red or Orange
Symbol: Burning House
Invoke to protect the home and for help with any kind of emergency that has to do with home such as a flood, fire, bankruptcy, infestation etc.

23 - Francis of Assisi
One of the best-known Saints, St. Francis walked away from a life of nobility to embrace poverty, charity, and devotion to the sacred Humanity of Christ. He founded the Order of Friars Minor (the Franciscans), which has given many Saints to the Church. He was known as a friend to animals, and many churches host a blessing of animals on his feast-day.
Feast: October 4
Candle Color: Brown
Invoke to petition for peace, conflict resolution and to gain spiritual wisdom. He helps to reveal and dismantle evil plots. He is also an environmentalist and is concerned with matters of ecology and conservation.

24 - Francis Xavier Cabrini
Francis Xavier was a student at the Paris University when he joined St. Ignatius of Loyola and became one of the first members of the Society of Jesus. He rapidly attained great holiness and, in obedience to his superiors, set out to preach the Gospel in the East Indies. His humility, patience, and charity made his missionary work prodigiously successful. Pope St. Pius X declared him the patron of Catholic missionary works.
Feast: December 30
Candle Color: White
Invoke to help with matters of immigration, with moving to another city or state or for matters pertaining to health, education or insurance.

25 - Gabriel the Archangel

Gabriel is one of three Archangels mentioned by name in Holy Scripture. He announced the mystery of the Incarnation to the prophet Daniel and to Zacharias, the father of St. John the Baptist. Finally he made the annunciation to the Virgin Mary and obtained her consent to become the Mother of God. He is also considered the Patron of communications workers.
Feast: March 24
Candle Color: Silver or Blue
Symbol: Trumpet or Lily
Invoke to communicate with a loved one or to interpret dreams.

26 – George, Patron of England

Little is known about this martyr of the Eastern Church, except that he suffered in the persecution of Diocletian. According to tradition, he was a member of one of the Roman legions. Devotion to him has always been widespread in the East, and after the Crusades it extended to the West when he was adopted as the patron Saint of England.
Feast: April 23
Candle Color: Red
Symbol: Slaying of a Dragon
Invoke to conquer fears, acquire courage and to overcome jealousy.

27 - Gerard Majella

St. Gerard became entered the Redemptorist Order at the age of 23. He had the abilities of levitation, bi-location, and the reading of consciences, and exhibited a charity and piety by which he received permission to counsel communities of women. He died of tuberculosis in 1755, and is the patron of expectant mothers.

Feast: October 16
Candle Color: White
Invoke to petition to become pregnant. He also helps the falsely accused be declared innocent. He also assists mediums, prophets, psychics and clairvoyants in seeing the truth.

28 - Helen of Jerusalem
Mother of the Emperor Constantine, St. Helen converted to Christianity after her son's victory at the Milvian Bridge, and on a pilgrimage to the Holy Land she uncovered the True Cross. She died in 330, and her sarcophagus now rests in the Vatican Museum.
Feast: August 18
Candle Color: Pink or Red
Symbol: Cross
Invoke to ask for the return of a strayed lover and to overcome sorrow, obsession and unhappiness. Her emblem is a cross.

29 - Ignatius of Loyola
At the age of 33 Ignatius abandoned the life of a courtier and a soldier and consecrated himself to the service of Christ and the Church. With some companions, he formed the Society of Jesus to carry out obediently any task which the Church might assign them. The society founded by him continues to this day, and Ignatius' *Spiritual Exercises* have led many people to holiness. He is the patron of spiritual retreats.
Feast: July 31
Candle Color: White
Symbol: Book and a Plum
Invoke to protect the house from burglary and evil spirits, to combat the enemies of the Church, and for conversion of those who have strayed from the Christian Faith.

30 - James the Greater the Apostle
St. James, with his brother St. John, left all to follow Jesus along with St. Peter. James was a witness to many of Jesus' miracles, and was first of the Apostles to suffer martyrdom, being beheaded in Jerusalem in 42.
Feast: July 25
Candle Color: Red
Symbol: Cockleshell
Invoke to clear obstacles from your path, conquer or remove enemies and for justice to prevail.

31 - Joan of Arc
The patroness of soldiers and of France, St. Joan of Arc was a peasant girl from Lorraine. Disguised as a boy, she went to the King of France and assisted him in achieving success after military success, restoring him to his kingdom. However, the French did little to thank her, as they did nothing to save her from the Burgundians, who sold her to the English, tried her as a heretic and burned her at the stake. She was canonized by Benedict XV in 1920.
Feast: May 30
Candle Color: Gray
Symbol: Suit of Armor
Invoke to petition her for spiritual strength, freedom from prisons of all kinds (emotional and otherwise) and for ways to overcome rivals and energies.

32 - John the Baptist
St. John the Baptist was Jesus' cousin, and son of the priest Zechariah. As an adult, he retired to the desert where he lived austerely while announcing the coming of the Messiah. He preached penitence at the river Jordan, and was beheaded for preaching against King Herod Antipas.
Feast: June 24 (Nativity), August 29 (Beheading)
Candle Color: Green.

Invoke to petition him for good luck, fertility, prosperity and protection from enemies.

33 - John Bosco
St. John Bosco founded the Salesian order for men and the Daughters of Mary Help of Christians for women. As a humble and poor priest he accomplished immense good for the Church in Italy and throughout the world in the nineteenth century. In particular, he undertook the care and education of poor children and, relying solely on the help of Divine Providence, raised great institutes to provide homes for them. He died in 1888 and was canonized in 1934.
Feast: January 31
Candle Color: Yellow
Invoke to petition him for favors for children, students and educational matters.

34 - Joseph, Spouse of the Virgin Mary
Next to the Blessed Virgin Mary, St. Joseph holds the highest dignity among all the Saints. He was the spouse of Mary, foster-father of Jesus Christ, and head of the Holy Family of Nazareth. To fit him for this exalted office, he was endowed with great holiness and virtue. Because of the assistance of Jesus and Mary at his deathbed, he is the patron of a happy death.
Feast: March 19
Candle Color: Yellow
Symbol: Lily, Pitcher with Loaf of Bread
Invoke for help with selling a home, finding job, for protection and a happy marriage.

35 - Joseph Sarto (Pope St. Pius X)
Born Joseph Sarto, St. Pius X was the son of the village postman at Riese in northern Italy. Throughout his career he was known for his zeal in the care of souls and his

activity in promoting Catholic social action. In particular, he was noted for his boundless generosity to the poor and afflicted, and the promotion of frequent and daily Communion even for the very young. He was beatified in 1951 by Pope Pius XII, who also canonized him on May 30, 1954.
Feast: September 3
Candle Color: White
Invoke to be granted favors by those in authority (such as a boss or government agency), for help in teaching the Faith to children, and for assistance against the enemies of Christianity

36 - Jude the Apostle
St. Jude, the brother of St. James the Less, is called the "brother of the Lord," because he was Jesus' cousin. Tradition has it that he preached the Gospel in Mesopotamia and Persia before ending his life by martyrdom.
Feast: October 28
Candle Color: Green, White, or Red
Symbol: Medal with the Face of Jesus, Staff
Invoke to petition for a miracle: for hopeless cases that seem impossible, to help with addictions or to help someone get out of jail.

37 - Lawrence
A native of Spain, St. Lawrence was archdeacon to Pope Sixtus II. After the Pope's martyrdom, he distributed to the poor all the possessions of the Church. This enraged the city's prefect, who then had St. Lawrence roasted to death on a gridiron. Lawrence bore this excruciating torture calmly and prayed constantly for the conversion of Rome. His death took place in 258.
Feast: August 10
Candle Color: Red

Symbol: Gridiron
Invoke to petition for a peaceful, happy home and family, for financial assistance and spiritual strength.

38 - Lazarus
St. Lazarus is the brother of Mary and Martha, whom Jesus raised back from the dead. In one tradition, he and his sisters went to France, where he became the first bishop of Marseilles before being martyred. Other traditions exist claiming he went to Syria or Lamaka, and his relics are in Constantinople today.
Feast: July 29
Candle Color: Yellow
Symbol: Pair of Crutches, Dog
Invoke to ask for help with sickness, disease, addictions, and better health and to obtain prosperity.

39 - Louis Bertrand
A Dominican priest, St. Louis was a gifted preacher and a missionary to South America where he displayed the gift of tongues while preaching to the many tribes there (i.e. he spoke in Spanish and they heard in their own languages).
Feast: October 9
Candle Color: White
Invoke for help learning languages and protection from evil, accidents, sickness and enemies. He is the one you invoke when children are possessed by spirits.

40 - Lucy
Lucy was reared in the Christian faith by her mother Eutychia, and she made a secret vow to consecrate herself to God as a virgin. Because of this, the young pagan who had been chosen as her husband denounced her to the authorities. After many torments, she perished by fire after she had foretold the early ending of the persecution of the Christians. She died in 304.

Feast: December 13
Candle Color: White
Invoke to ask her to help with insoluble or impossible problems, depression, and protection from the evil eye or astral attack, to help you to find the right lawyer and to conquer temptations or addictions.

41 - Maria Goretti
St. Maria Goretti (1890-1902) is the youngest of Saints canonized in the Catholic Church. She was born in 1890 in Corinaldo, Italy, and was mortally wounded in 1902 while resisting a sexual assault. She died from that assault, but not before forgiving her assailant. Canonized by Pope Pius XII in 1950, she is now the patroness of youth, young women, and victims of rape.
Feast: July 6
Candle Color: Pink
Invoke for fidelity in marriage, help with an abusive or battering male partner and a pardon from the death penalty.

42 - Martha
St. Martha, the sister of Lazarus and Mary Magdalen, was frequently hostess to our Savior and was especially loved by him. Of her later life no details are known although one tradition says she died in France.
Feast: July 29
Candle Color: Green or White
Symbol: Dragon
Invoke to ask for aid with financial problems, the necessities of life, to bring a lover closer, to keep a husband or boyfriend faithful, to subdue or conquer romantic rivals or enemies or bring a new love.

43 - Martin Caballero (St. Martin of Tours)
Born in 315 in the province of Pannonia, St. Martin was the son of a pagan army official who was intolerant of the New

Religion. Martin converted to Christianity of his own volition, but before he was baptized he was consigned a soldier in the Roman army, making him the patron of soldiers. He remained constant in his faith, and was eventually baptized. He eventually became bishop of Tours, and lived a life of poverty and humility until his death in the late fourth century.
Feast: November 11
Candle Color: Red or White
Symbol: Torn Cape and Sword
Invoke to ask for protection from evil, to rescue someone from evil influences and/or to draw customers to your business. Petition him for money, luck prosperity.

44 - Martin De Porres
St. Martin was born in Lima, Peru, and in 1594 entered the Dominican Order as a lay brother at the age of fifteen, where he worked several jobs (a barber amongst them) and devoted himself to the path of Green Martyrdom. He possessed spiritual wisdom, and in his life of holiness God granted him many gifts, including aerial flight and bi-location. He is the patron Saint of barbers.
Feast: November 3
Candle Color: Purple or White
Symbol: Broom and a Crucifix
Invoke to bring harmony to your household. You can also petition him for better health and increased financial security.

45 - Michael the Archangel
St. Michael the Archangel leads the hosts of God in their battle with Satan and he is the special protector of the Church. He who was responsible for throwing the devil and the renegade angels into Hell, and he is commonly invoked as the special protector of Christians from any and all dangers.

Feast: September 29
Candle Color: Red
Symbol: Sword
Invoke for protection against the enemies of Christianity, against danger of all types, for courage, and for victory in battle.

46 - Monica
St. Monica was the mother of St. Augustine. She devoted herself to works of charity and piety after the death of her husband. She prayed and worked constantly on her son's behalf, until she secured his conversion by St. Ambrose of Milan.
Feast: May 4
Candle Color: White
Invoke to draw back those who have strayed from Christianity.

47 - Olaf Haraldsson
The patron of carvers, kings, Norway and Scandinavia, St. Olaf was born a pagan and while a-viking, was baptized at Rouen, France, at the age of 18. He returned to Norway to unify the land and purge paganism from his realm, while the Danes set to take the kingdom from him. He was killed at the Battle of Stiklestad in 1031. The details of the many miracles that led to his canonization are reported in the *Heimskringla* of Snorri Sturlusson.
Feast: July 29
Candle Color: Red or Purple
Symbol: Lion with Battle-Axe in Forepaws
Invoke to become a strong ruler and for help in difficult marriages.

48 - Patrick
The loyalty of the Irish people to the Faith and to the Church is a great monument to Saint Patrick, their national

Apostle. His labors in Ireland were accompanied and made fruitful by his extraordinary gifts of prayer and penance. In later years Ireland became known as the Island of Saints and Scholars.
Feast: March 17
Candle Color: White
Symbol: Shamrock
Invoke for prosperity, luck, spiritual wisdom, and guidance in difficult matters.

49 - Paul the Apostle
St. Paul, the "Apostle to the Gentiles," was born Saul of Tarsus around 10 A.D. and was received his training from the great rabbi Gamaliel. At first a persecutor of the Church, he had a vision of Jesus while on the road to Damascus, where he instantly converted. He was martyred in Rome on the same day as St. Peter.
Feast: January 25 and June 29
Candle Color: Blue or Red
Symbol: Sword
Invoke for courage, patience, to overcome opposition and settle disturbed conditions in the home.

50 - Peregrine Laziosi
St. Peregrine was born to a wealthy family in Forli, Italy, and joined the Servire Order after an incident with St. Phillip Benizi, where he observed silence and solitude as much as possible. He was later afflicted with cancer of the foot, and was miraculously cured through prayer. Today he is considered the patron Saint of cancer patients.
Feast: none
Candle Color: White
Symbol: Shepherd's Crook Tied to a Purse
Invoke to petition him for help with cancer.

51 - Peter the Apostle
Simon Peter, the first of the Apostles, was named by Jesus "the Rock on which I shall build my Church." (Matthew 16:18). A leader in the early Christianity, St. Peter became known as the "Apostle to the Jews," and wrought many miracles while guiding the Church in her first decades. He established the two most ancient Patriarchates at Antioch and Rome. St. Peter was crucified upside-down at Rome in 62.
Feast: January 18 and June 29
Candle Color: Red or White
Symbol: Two Crossed Keys
Invoke to petition him to remove obstacles, business success, strength, courage, forgiveness and good fortune.

52 - Philomena
Nothing is known of St. Philomena's life, save that she was martyred when she was 14 years old. Her tomb was found in the catacomb of St. Priscilla, and she is the only Saint ever canonized based solely on the power of her intercession.
Feast: none
Candle Color: Pink or Green
Symbol: Anchor
Invoke to help with desperate situations, problems with children, unhappiness in the home, the sick, selling real estate, food for the poor and mental illness. Philomena is a favorite of single mothers.

53 - Raphael the Archangel
Raphael, one of *"the seven spirits that stand before the throne of God"* (Tobit 12:15; Revelation 1:4, 3:1, 4:5, 5:6), was sent to guide young Tobias on his journey and to heal the blindness of his father Tobit. He is invoked especially for the healing of infirmities mental physical.
Feast: October 24

Candle Color: Pink
Symbol: Pilgrim's Staff
Invoke for a safe journey, for protection against ill health and disease, and to heal or cure.

54 - Raymond Nonnatus
St. Raymond Nonnatus undertook a voyage to Africa to redeem Christian captives. He was imprisoned and mutilated when he surrendered himself as a pledge for the ransom of some prisoners. Later he was created Cardinal but died at Cardona near Barcelona when on his way to Rome.
Feast: August 31
Devotional Color: Red
Symbol: Monstrance and Palm with Three Crowns
Invoke to prevent gossip, false accusation and for a happy and peaceful home.

55 - Rita of Cascia
The patroness of hopeless causes and the impossible, St. Rita suffered for eighteen years as a battered wife until the day her husband was killed in a brawl. Again, against hopeless odds, she was finally accepted into the Augustinian Order where she lived out her days a nun and received wounds on her forehead resembling a crown of thorns. She died on May 22, 1457.
Feast: May 22
Devotional Color: White
Symbol: Crown of Thorns
Invoke to assist with an abusive relationship, to relieve loneliness, for deliverance from evil and for spiritual fortitude and strength

56 - Rocco
Rocco (Roch in France, Roque in Spain) was the son of the governor of Montpellier, France, who went on a pilgrimage

to Rome and cared for the victims of a plague afflicting Italy, where he was said to affect a great many cures. When he returned to France, he was imprisoned on suspicion of being a spy in pilgrim's clothing. He died in prison, and after his death it was discovered that he was the governor's son. His intercession is invoked against pestilence and plague, and he is also the patron of invalids.
Feast: August 16
Candle Color: White
Symbol: Dog
Invoke to restore health and to be protected from contagious diseases.

57 - Sebastian
St. Sebastian was an officer in the Imperial Guard in Rome. Because of his assistance to those punished for their faith, he was sentenced to death in 288 by shooting with arrows. He was miraculously cured of his wounds, and so Diocletian ordered that he should be beaten to death with clubs.
Feast: January 20
Candle Color: Red
Symbol: Arrows
Invoke to petition for justice, to overcome rivals, remove obstacles from your path, success and good fortune.

58 - Therese of Lisieux
St. Therese was born in Alencon and educated in Lisieux. At the age of fifteen she entered the Carmel of Lisieux and nine years later she died there in December, 1897. After her death she has become one of the great popular Saints of our time. The characteristic of her holiness was her "little way" of striving by humility and love to obtain that child-like simplicity of heart which Jesus loves, to be a "Little Flower" in the garden of the Lord. Because of her prayers for missionaries in foreign lands, St. Therese was named by

Pope Pius XI as the special patroness of all Catholic Missions.
Feast: October 3
Devotional Color: Yellow
Symbol: Bouquet of Roses
Invoke to be loved by all, for popularity, for help with addiction and alcoholism, for protection from black magic and to restore faith.

59 - Thomas Aquinas
Perhaps the greatest theologian and philosopher in Church history, St. Thomas was born at Rocca Secca and educated at the abbey of Monte Cassino. He entered the Oder of Preachers (Dominicans) in the face of strong opposition from his family, and by vigorous resistance to temptation he attained angelic purity. He was gifted with prodigious power of mind, and during his lifetime he was renowned as a professor of philosophy and theology in Paris. His writings on the sacred sciences offer such clarity and depth that they formed the basis of all theological teaching for centuries afterward.
Feast: March 7
Candle Color: White
Invoke to improve concentration and memory, for understanding, for mental stamina and to help pass exams.

Prayers in Honor of the Saints
To open any Catholic prayerbook at random, or even a superficial search of the internet, is to find a great number of prayers to the Saints. There are candles and oils blessed in their names, objects blessed on their feast-days, and prayers asking them for help in some or other matter.

The greater portion of a Christian magician's work involves the Saints and Angels, and fortunately one doesn't need to memorize books filled with long prayers and orations. The

Saints and Angels are happier with a prayer that comes from your own heart than one memorized from a book.

Even so, you may wish to turn to such prayers as examples for how to compose your own. Our grandparents' childhood prayerbooks are filled with examples, and websites such as *Treasury of Latin Prayers* provide examples in both Latin and English (http://www.preces-latinae.org/index.htm). A fairly large collection of prayers can also be found in the appendix of my *The Things We Do: Ways of the Holy Benedetta* (2007, THAVMA Publications).

When using these prayers to petition the Saints, it's important to remember that it's God alone who answers our prayers, while the Saints are asked to advocate our cause to God. The general procedure is to light a candle of that Saint's color and pray first to God to take the matter under his wing, then to the Saint to intercede on our behalf. There will be several examples of this in Chapter Seven.

IV. CANDLES, RELICS, MEDALS, TALISMANS

For a book that's supposed to be about candle magic, we really haven't done much to discuss candles, now have we? Have no fear, gentle reader, for now that's about to change!

In the work of a Christian magician, the sacramentals play a very important part. In the Baltimore Catechism, Lesson 36, we are told that *"Sacramentals are holy things or actions of which the Church makes use to obtain for us from God, through her intercession, spiritual and temporal favors."* (Question #469, 1941 edition)

These holy things or actions involve prayers, blessed objects, and sacred actions which rouse us to deepen our faith in God and the power of His Church. Prayers, blessings, holy water, relics, medals, blessed candles, and even magical operations can all be called sacramentals.

With this understanding, we should keep in mind that everything discussed in this chapter will be discussed from the viewpoint that all sacred works are sacramentals, because we speak here only of operations that glorify God by inviting Him to display his power in our lives here on earth for the betterment of His faithful. When we see God's wondrousness and graciousness towards us, it shows us that He cares about us, and thus our love and faith in Him are strengthened in turn. This is the true source and the true end of the Christian magician's work: *ad majorem Dei gloriam*!

Candles as a Sacramental
The use of candles, as stated in Chapter I, goes back to the earliest days of the Church. As the candles' light became a symbol of dispelling darkness, it eventually became

customary for the priest to bless candles for the faithful to bring into their homes. The blessing itself, as found in the pre-Vatican II *Roman Ritual*, explicitly charges the candles with to drive evil away from any place where they're lit or even placed. When the Church turns these creatures of wax into weapons of protection, she makes these candles a sacramental intended to signify (through their success at this task) God's loving and Fatherly protection, thus building up and reinforcing faith and love for Him.

This can be a powerful sacramental, and the "powers of darkness" which are mentioned don't necessarily need to be the demons and legions of hell; when we use these candles magically, to us these forces can be any obstacle which keeps us from obtaining the goal we set out to accomplish; perhaps the biggest stumbling-block can be our own doubts, negative thoughts, and emotions. As such, the blessing of the Church for candles should be given to all candles used in our magical rites, regardless of the purpose for which we are working.

As to the purposes themselves, people generally tend to perform magic for one of four intentions. In order of frequency, these objectives are: love, money, health, and protection. Most other things classify into one of these four categories, so we can think of these as the "four basic food groups."

If you so desire, you can place a blessing on these candles not only to protect you from harm or defeat any obstacles to manifesting your intentions, you can also bless them to assist in bringing about your goals. This means the blessing will be defensive in that it defends you against obstacles and clears them out of the way, and also proactive because it works to bring your goals into manifestation.

When blessing a candle, we always begin with usual versicles and responses that go with any blessing:

V. Our help is in the name of the Lord.
R. Who made heaven and earth.
V. The Lord be with you.
R. And with your spirit.

If you work with an assistant, you would say the parts marked "V" (for "versicle") while your assistant says the parts labeled "R" (for "response"). If working alone, you say all the parts yourself.

After the versicles, you say "Let us pray," and then hold at least one hand over the candles while saying the prayer of blessing, making the sign of the Cross over them every time you encounter a "plus sign." (+)

Lord Jesus Christ, Son of the living God, +bless these candles at our humble request. Endow them by the power of the holy +Cross, O Lord, and by your heavenly blessing. You gave them to humankind to dispel darkness; let the blessing they receive by the sign of the holy +Cross be so powerful that the princes of darkness and all their legions will tremble and depart from wherever they are lighted or placed. May they flee in fear and never more dare to disturb those who serve you, almighty God, who live and reign forever and ever.
R. Amen.

If you're only blessing the candles for protection or for general use as altar/mensa candles, then you would stop here and sprinkle the candles with Holy Water. If you're blessing the candles for another intention, then you again say "Let us pray" and one of the additional prayers below before sprinkling with Holy Water.

For Love (marriage, friendship, reconciliation, etc.):
Almighty everlasting God, through whose love the human race was redeemed; I ask humbly that you will again pour your +blessing into these candles, and bless them to bring me the lover I desire. You who live and reign forever and ever.
R. Amen.

For Money (success, luck, etc.):
NOTE: This prayer serves an example of how Kabbalistic invocations can be fit into Christian blessings.

Hear me, Holy Lord, Father Almighty, eternal God, whose name is El when you preside over the Sphere of Hesed; +bless this candle that it shall manifest much money into the life of N., and send your holy Archangel Tsadkiel from the heavens, along with the Angelic Order of the Hashmalim or Dominations, and your Intelligence Iofiel, that they may physically manifest much money into the life of N., who lives in the Sphere of Malchus, the orb of the Earth. To this end, may the above-named be helped by your Archangel Sandalfon, the Order of the Eshim or the Church Triumphant, and every entity and power of the Spheres of Malchus and the Element of Earth. May the purse of N. be replete with gold, silver, and every type of money legal in the United States of America, may always the purse of N. be full. Through our Lord Jesus Christ, your Son, who lives and reigns with you in the unity of the Holy Spirit, one God, forever and ever.
R. Amen.

For Health (of the throat):
God, almighty and all-mild, by your Word alone you created all things, and willed that that same Word take flesh in order to redeem mankind; you are great and immeasurable, awesome and praiseworthy, a worker of

marvels. Hence in professing his faith in you the glorious martyr and bishop, Blaise, did not fear any manner of torment but gladly accepted the palm of martyrdom. For this you gave him many gifts, amongst them the power to heal all ailments of the throat. We now implore your majesty to overlook our guilt and consider only his merits and intercession, to +bless and +sanctify, and impart your grace to these candles. Let all people of faith whose necks are touched with them be healed of every illness of the throat, and once they've been restored, let them give thanks to you and praise your glorious name which is blessed forever; through Our Lord Jesus Christ Thy Son, who lives and reigns with you in the unity of the Holy Ghost, God, forever and ever.
R. Amen.

For Health (fertility, childbearing, disease, injury, etc.): Lord Jesus Christ, Savior and healer of the human race, in memory of the woman who touch the hem of thy garment that she may be healed of the flowing of her blood; +bless these candles that, in the spirit of mercy which thou hast shown to many others, so also wilt thou heal whomsoever may keep these candles, or for whom they may be lit. You who live and reign forever and ever. *R*. Amen.

After saying the prayer corresponding to your specific purpose, the candles are sprinkled with Holy Water, while you say nothing. In sprinkling an object this way, the Church "baptizes" it, dedicating it to the service of Christ.

Types of Candles
Now that we've discussed blessed candles as a sacramental and given blessings to dedicate them for the four major magical purposes, let's talk about the different types of candles and how we can use them.

Here's the deal. Some of the things I say in this section may greatly differ from what most people do in some areas, while in others it may not. That's because in books on candle magic, authors tend to write about what works for *them*, and I'm no exception. As you go further in your study and practice with candles, you too will find the methods that work best for you.

1. Tea Lights
The most basic type of candle is the tea light, a small wax candle in a metal container. They're easy to come by, cost-effective, and convenient because they leave no wax to clean up. I buy them in bulk and use them by placing them in colored votive glasses. On average, they last about 4-6 hours, and so they're best used as offerings before praying a Rosary or making a request that's not life-altering. I generally burn two at a time, since I place two small votive glasses before an image of each Saint to whom I make a petition.

Votive candles could be used for this same purpose and with the same effectiveness, except you'll likely end up with wax to clean up. In fact cleanup is the reason I prefer tea lights.

2. Tapers
The second type of candle is the taper. These can be the dinner tapers found at almost any store, and I also use the word for the "straight" (non-tapering) candles that are also easily available. They come in varying lengths, widths, and colors, and are the type of candles that most authors discuss when talking about candle magic. I prefer these as altar/mensa candles, and for works where a candle is only burned for an hour or two each day.

For those interested in using straight candles but aren't so enthusiastic about dripping wax, you can get candle followers (available at church supply stores and home interior websites) and place them on top of the candle. For tapers, you can also find drip protectors that collect wax at the bottom of the candle; they look like glass saucers with a hole in the center.

3. Figure Candles

The next step up from tapers would be figure candles, which are shaped to resemble a naked man or woman. These are found in Pagan or New Age stores, and they come in a variety of colors. Use them to represent either yourself or the person for (or on) whom you're working, and if you use a figure candle, it should be in the main color of the work in question.

In my own practice, I rarely if ever use these (maybe once in the past 16 years), and tend to view them as no different in function from taper or straight candles. I've also noticed a tendency to drip wax everywhere, and you've probably figured out that I'm not too fond of having to clean up the mess.

4. 5-Day /7-Day & 14-Day Candles

These are the large candles seen on the votive rack at church, and you can find cheaply-made colored ones in grocery and dollar stores. As the name implies, these candles can burn for 5, 7, or 14 days until they burn themselves out. Speaking from personal experience, the cheaply-made ones tend to last 5 days, the ones at church 7, and the ones made for sanctuary lamps 14.

My personal preference would be the ones you find at church supply (and some New Age) stores, which consist of a plastic-encased candle (the "cartridge") placed inside a "globe" of colored glass. The cartridges you find at church supply and religious supply stores tend to be the best quality; they burn smoothly and consistently, with a minimum of black smoke or sparking.

The price for globes and cartridges can vary widely depending on where you buy them. You're usually better off if you can find them in religious supply shops, as church supply stores tend to be exorbitant with their prices. I suggest shopping around to find where you can get the best deal.

In my personal practice, I use these candles when something big needs to be done, or when help is needed quickly and powerfully. I don't know the reason with certainty, but I've seen results come faster with these than with any other type of candle.

5. Devil and Skull Candles
I've never used these, and mention them simply because they exist. According to some exponents of Rootwork and Hoodoo, these candles are used to break particularly strong curses. Beyond that I have no comment.

6. Soy Candles
In recent years, there has been an increasing interest in the environmentally-friendly soy candle. These candles can be white or colored, come in glass jars, and have an exceptionally long burning time, such as 40 hours for a four-ounce jar! From a practical standpoint, soy wax has a very low melting point of 125°, meaning you can dip your fingers into the candle while it's burning and not even feel a thing (I'd rather you didn't do this, though; the flame can still burn you!).

If you get them from the right place, these candles can be scented very strongly and can take the place of oils or incenses. Provided the makers kept a sensible scent-to-wax ratio, you'll find no black smoke coming from the candle and no soot left on the glass, thus enabling the jar to be refilled time and again. Basically the soy candle is perfectly adapted to magical use.

7. Light Bulbs
Back in February of '99, I tried an experiment to see whether light bulbs could work in the place of candles. I put a green light bulb (for money) in a lamp in my room and kept it lit, never turning it off, even when I went to sleep. The experiment turned out to be quite successful, and it's always good when a little extra money finds its way into the home.

When we discussed color in Chapter II, we described several experiments that made use of colored light, so that the subject would be saturated with color. Now when burning candles, what we really have is a yellowish-white flame coming from a painted piece of wax or glass. Yet when we use a light bulb, the whole room becomes saturated with color; the color becomes even more a part of us and our designs.

If you use light bulbs, I'd recommend using the 25-watt "party bulbs" that can be found just about anywhere. They're great because they come in a large assortment of colors, and at 25 watts they give sufficient without an electric bill that breaks the bank!

Working with the Candles
Now that we have described the different types of candles, we can briefly discuss methods for working with them. In general, the type, size, and color of the candles you will use

are a matter of personal preference, though on your altar or mensa you should have two white taper/straight candles for your "altar candles." These are used to show that you only want your work to succeed through Christ's power and His intervention.

On the far center side of the mensa you should have a standing cross of crucifix, signifying that it's the Precious Blood of Jesus Christ that gives us power to command the spirits and the elements, and it is through Him that we are made members of the Church and of the Communion of Saints, whose help we now ask in manifesting our designs. Optionally, in front of your Crucifix you may choose to have a red altar candle, representing the power of Christ's Blood. It's also suggested to keep a bowl or jar of holy water nearby.

Below is a picture of what the basic mensa setup would look like:

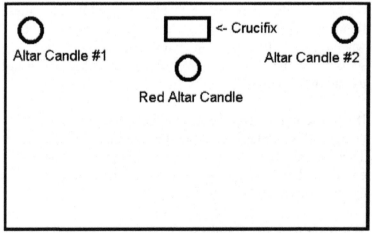

Figure 4-1: Basic Altar/Mensa Setup

Any other candles that you use are determined by the type of operation you wish to accomplish, and are placed on the mensa according to your personal discretion. The candles can represent you or the person on whom you're working, they can represent the Saint with whom you're working, or they can represent different aspects of the situation.

In general, when a Saint (or more than one Saint) is being petitioned, you would find an image of him or her and have it on your mensa. In my practice, I have some 5"x7" picture frames that I use, and I find an image of the Saint(s) on the internet; yes, modern technology makes everything easier! I then format it in to fit a 5 x 7 frame, print it on card stock, bless it, and frame it. Afterwards I take two votive glasses of that Saint's color and put tea lights in each one.

When lighting a candle to a Saint, one could anoint the candle with an appropriate oil. For St. Joseph, for example, you could pour two drops of lily oil onto each tea light, or use rose for the Virgin Mary. You can place a garlic clove in front of St. Michael, and so on and so on.

Once we've selected (not yet lit) our candles and have our images set up, we may dip our right hands in Holy Water and cross ourselves, and then state our Declaration of Intent in our own words. It doesn't matter what you say here, but it should be short, to-the-point, and totally honest with God and with yourself.

Once you have made your Declaration, you light the three altar candles in this order, while saying the following phrases:
Red Candle: «**Per Christum**» (Through Christ)
Left Candle: «**Ex Miséria**» (Out of misery)
Right Candle: «**Et in Glóriam!**» (And into Glory!)

There is a potent symbolism here. In doing magic, we are looking to be delivered from the misery of our present situation and into the glory of successful results, and so we enforce this passage in our minds, along with the fact that we'll make this transition through Christ. Just as through him that we were passed out of the misery of Original Sin and into the Glory of Eternal Salvation.

The next step is to anoint our candles with oils representing either the Saints or our problems, and there are several ways to do this: one school of thought teaches that we anoint our candles from the center up, and again from the center down; another school of thought teaches that we rub the oil on the candle in a twisting motion, similar to screwing the candle into the oil; and with 5- or 7- day candles, you would plunge a screwdriver into the wax and create a hole, which in turn you would fill with the oil.

Speaking of oils, there are a lot of them out there, and it would be a task to catalogue them all. My own system doesn't really make use of "Hot Foot" or "Money Drawing" oil, but instead focuses on the flower or plant symbolic of the Saint, and uses the essential from that plant.

Once your candles have been anointed, it's time to light them. You would begin by lighting the candle which represents you or the person on whom you're working, and say: **"This is N., who needs Almighty God, by the intercession of St. N.N., bring to N. the gift of** *(insert intention here)."*

You would then proceed to light the other candles on the mensa (if any), briefly identifying what these candles represent and what you hope to accomplish through them. When lighting the candles representing a Saint or before a

Saint's image, say: "**O glorious St. N., whose holy life won for you the grace of heaven, humbly I ask that you accept this offering of lights (and food/oil/etc.), and intercede on behalf of my petitions before the Father. Through Christ our Lord. Amen.**"

After your candles are lit, you may meditate, pray, visualize, or whatever it is that you've decided to do for this operation. When you're done, leave all votive, tealight, or 7-day candles burning, while snuffing out any other types of candles. Finally, would extinguish your altar candles while saying:
Red: «**In Christo**» (In Christ)
Left: «**Omnis Terra**» (May all the Earth)
Right: «**Instaurétur**» (Be Restored)

Then you would say a prayer of thanks in your own words, thanking God for bringing your desire and speaking as if it had already been fulfilled (this is a show of faith). Finally, you make the Sign of the Cross over yourself, and put all thoughts of the working out of your mind. Do something mundane like make a sandwich or play a video game, and know that your desire is now in good hands.

Relics and Medals
Amongst the sacramentals which the Church provides are relics and medals, both of which connect us not only to the Saints but also to the intercessory power of the Church.

<u>Relics (Reliquiae)</u>
In the early centuries of the Church, worship services were held over the tombs of the Martyrs, both in memory of their blood shed for their faith in Christ, and also that the Martyr would intercede for those present; in later centuries this custom was preserved by the use of an "Altar Stone" and an "Antimension" in the East, both of which enclose the

first-class relics of at least two martyred Saints. In a very graphic and physical way, the Mass has, in all times, been linked not only between God and Church Militant, but with the Church Triumphant as well.

First-class relics (i.e. a Saint's body parts) aren't always easy to come by, and some people may understandably be squeamish about the concept. In the absence of a first-class relic, however, for our purposes it works to obtain a "relic card," essentially a Holy Card that comes with either a piece of the Saint's clothing or something known to have been blessed by the Saint. These are called "second-class" and "third-class" relics, respectively.

Through the use of relics, we create a link between ourselves and the Saint(s) we invoke, the same way that we would use a Holy Card or an image. The difference is that a relic is more personal the Saint, and so it creates a much more powerful link with him or her.

We have a few options when using relics, and the primary place is on your mensa. On the one hand, we could simply place them on top of the mensa, next to the candles representing the Saint. On the other hand, we could purchase a reliquary from eBay and place that on the mensa, giving an added sense of dignity.

The third option is to enclose a relic in your mensa permanently. I would only recommend this with your Patron Saint or a Saint with whom you have a strong rapport. You could enclose the relic(s) in a small wooden box (about 6" x 6" x 1") and fasten the box to the bottom of your mensa (or, if you're really good at woodworking, incorporate the box into the mensa's top). Your options are limitless, and this effectively consecrates your mensa to the Saint.

Medals (Numismata)
In Catholic culture, it's common to find people wearing a medal of a Patron Saint around their neck, or to hang a St. Christopher medal over their car's rear-view mirror. Protestants have historically accused Catholics of being "superstitious" because of this, yet many modern Protestants have an attachment to oil to drive out demons, or "speaking words of victory" to improve their lives.

Practically speaking, a medal is commonly used as a petition for protection (i.e. St. Christopher or St. Benedict medals), though more technically we could look at the medal as useful for linking our magical operations with the outside world.

For example, if we're looking to find a wife or husband, we burn candles to St. Therese of Lisieux on our mensa. However, just sitting home alone will not bring us a potential spouse; we have to go out there and put ourselves around other people. So before we go out, we would wear a medal of St. Therese and ask her to help us. Through the medal serving as a reminder of her intercession, she'll help us find and discern the right person once we meet them.

As the candles connect our work to the power of God Almighty, and relics connect our work with the Church Triumphant, it's the medals that can connect our work with the world at large.

Talismans (Amulets and Seals)
Though the word "talisman" is not used favorably by Christians, the word could be considered in various ways. In one sense, it's merely a symbolic representation of your desire. That is, you write what you want to happen in symbols and/or words. Writing "I want money" or "I want

people in school to like me," for example, is a basic kind of talisman.

In practice, the best talismans are those into which you put the most of your own energy, meaning the ones you construct by yourself. You can use colors, symbols, lines, words (and languages) all to your liking, provided that to you they resonate with the meaning and the energy that represents your desire. When used, they can be placed under candles or worn similarly to medals, they can be carried in the pocket or purse, or even given to the person that you wish to affect.

You can make talismans out of any substance you feel appropriate. You can use paper or parchment, gold or silver, or even paint your symbolism on flower petals. There are really no limits, and with the great variety of options available, it would be impossible here to discuss all of them in depth.

V. MAGIC AND THE ROSARY

Much has been written about the Rosary, and perhaps the best such work would be *The Secret of the Rosary* by St. Louis de Montfort. In this book St. Louis discusses the Rosary, its prayers, its spirituality, and its devotion as a powerful help in attaining heaven. He also mentions the "promises of the Rosary" which include obtaining whatever one asks in prayer.

Whether one has read St. Louis' book, it's a safe bet to assume most Christians have heard of the Rosary. Whether they practice it regularly or view it as a superstition, at least they know that it exists.

The basic layout of the Rosary consists of fifteen "Mysteries," which are further broken down into three groups of five Mysteries each – Joyful, Sorrowful, and Glorious – and the prayers consist mostly of the Our Father, Hail Mary, and Glory Be. It's very easy to learn and is the core practice found in a great deal of prayer works and novenas.

Some Magical Uses
In magical use, the Rosary can be one of the most powerful weapons at our disposal. Through the promises made by Our Lady to St. Dominic and to Bl. Alan de la Roche, it's through the Rosary that we gain victory over our enemies and the fruit of receiving the things for which we pray.

In the chapter called the "Twenty-Seventh Rose," St. Louis lists seven benefits to praying the Rosary:

1 it gradually brings us a perfect knowledge of Jesus Christ;
2 it purifies our souls from sin;
3 it gives us victory over all our enemies;

4 it makes the practice of virtue easy;
5 it sets us on fire with the love of our Lord;
6 it enriches us with graces and merits;
7 it supplies us with what is needed to pay all our debts to God and to our fellow-men, and finally, it obtains all kinds of graces from God.

In essence, it could be said the Rosary is the ultimate weapon a Christian can use not only in seeking to practice virtue and be illumined in the Faith necessary to enter Heaven, but also as the key for opening the gates of Heaven so actual graces may rain down from God's throne and shower upon us here on the earth below.

Now, to a practicing Christian magician that last sentence takes on a special meaning, for the Rosary in and of itself is a powerful sacramental. In conjunction with candleburning operations, the Rosary can help to accelerate the mobilization of the powers of Heaven on our behalf.

This is why numerous Rosary novenas exist, and the longest is perhaps the longest being the 54-day Novena to Our Lady of Pompeii, which I always recommend to people in serious necessity. In this novena, one prays the Rosary for 27 days, praying the Mysteries assigned to each day, while in petition for that which he desires. For the next 27 days, he prays the Rosary while giving thanks for having received it, regardless of whether he really has received it or not. A little faith goes a long way, and this last half of the novena is the great show of faith and confidence.

Not only this novena, but any other can also be incorporated into our magical work. A simple example would be setting up the mensa with the altar candles, an image of whatever Saint you wish to petition, and the candle which represents the color either of that Saint or of your petition. You would then start by making your Declaration of Intent, and asking Almighty God to intervene on your behalf and grant your request. Next you pray the Rosary in whatever manner you normally do (sitting, stand, kneeling, etc.), while imagining your request as having been granted, or – if you don't have a vivid visual imagination – by repeating to yourself over and over again that your request has been granted.

In my own usage, I use the following prayer after completing the Rosary:

"O most Sorrowful and Immaculate Blessed Virgin Mary, Mother of God and Mother of men, thou who wast found worthy to carry God himself in thy womb, and thou who has crushed him who is at once the enemy of God and man in common under thy heel. Humbly do I, N., approach thee, through these Joyful (*or* Sorrowful. *or* Glorious) Mysteries of this thy Most Holy Rosary, asking that this offering may be acceptable to thee, and that thou wilt earnestly intercede on behalf of my petitions before the Father, namely that (*here name your petitions*). Through our Lord Jesus Christ thy Son, who with the Father liveth and reigneth in the unity of the Holy Ghost, God, forever and ever. Amen."

This prayer grew from a habit that I had of talking to the Blessed Mother after finishing my daily Rosary, and didn't actually take a concrete form until 1998 or so. In fact, this could be elaborated *ad infinitum*, because the part that says "here name your petitions" is usually a long talk or meditation, which changes according to time, feeling, and circumstance. In other words, I advocate for form with flexibility.

As to the Mysteries of the Rosary themselves, it's commonly said they pertain to the three phases of the mystical life: the Sorrowful Mysteries to the purgative, Joyful to the illuminative, and the Glorious to the unitive life. They are also attributed to a certain "spiritual fruit," or virtue such as humility, charity, self-control, perseverance, and so on. I give a fuller description of the Mysteries, their virtues, and their relation to the spiritual life in the Epilogue to my *The Magic of Catholicism*.

These virtues are important for magicians, and students of the occult will recognize the necessity of these virtues to any effective magical practice, and students of religion will at once recognize the necessity of these virtues for any kind of effective devotional or mystical life.

On a similar vein, it can be said that the three groups of Mysteries tend to "stack on" to one another, as each group introduces new spiritual fruits and new virtues, doing so by building on the foundation laid in the group that came before it. For example, in the Third Joyful Mystery, we seek to be indifferent to the physical world and its influences upon us. In the Second Sorrowful, we seek to control our lower (physical) natures. And in the Second Glorious, we have conquered the world's influences and our physical natures and are looking upward to Heaven, our true home.

This way, each set of Mysteries enriches and enhances those that came before. The Joyful Mysteries are generally concerned with implanting into our souls a particular virtue (e.g. humility), the Sorrowfuls with excising the opposing vice (e.g. pride), and the Glorious with showing us the rewards of that virtue (e.g. Gifts of the Holy Ghost). A small amount of examination will enable the reader to crack the system, so there's no need to expand upon it in further detail here.

Magical Purposes and the Mysteries
The Joyful Mysteries (Mysteria Gaudiosa)
It should also be noted that each of the Mysteries is associated with one or other purpose. The First Joyful Mystery, the **Annunciation**, is associated with humility and acceptance of the divine will. That the Annunciation is the beginning of Jesus' journey in the flesh connects it with the beginning of one's spiritual journey, or beginnings or journeys in general.

The **Visitation** is associated with the spiritual fruit of charity, and as such is connected with works of love, harmony, friendship, and also of sacrificing of one's time and comfort for the sake of others. This is exemplified by the fact that Mary was pregnant, and for six months of her pregnancy she worked around Elizabeth's house and gave of herself so that her cousin may be more comfortable.

The **Nativity**, the Mystery where God manifests on earth in physical form, brings the spiritual fruit of indifference to the world and its physical conditions. St. Ignatius, in his *Spiritual Exercises*, tells us that we should become indifferent to heat or cold, wealth or poverty, and so on and so forth, and while praying the Rosary back on the Feast of the Immaculate Conception in 2000, I remember meditating upon this Mystery and I heard a voice saying to me: "Indifference is power." I interpreted the as saying that when we are passionate or care inordinately about something or someone, then we allow ourselves to be controlled. Yet, when we are indifferent to that person or thing, we can become impervious to its influences, and in fact we can work ourselves into being in a position of control.

When the time prescribed by the Law had come, the infant Jesus was presented in the temple, in obedience to Divine

Law. Obedience as a virtue is connected with piety and spiritual love, which are the purposes for which God made man: "To know Him, to serve Him, and to love Him." Through obedience to the Law, we grow in our relationship with God and in our own personal spirituality. Thus this Mystery also figures into all operations where you would wish to grow or expand something.

The Fifth Joyful Mystery, the **Finding in the Temple**, centers on the episode in Luke's Gospel where Jesus was left behind in the Temple and confounded the Priests and the Doctors with his knowledge and discourse about God. When Mary and St. Joseph finally found him and asked what he was doing, he simply responded he was about "my Father's business." The spiritual fruit of this Mystery is conversion to Christ-ward, with Christ as the Sun around which our spiritual lives are in perpetual orbit. Many of us are in a distant orbit around that Sun, separating ourselves through sin and self-interest. This Mystery also contains another layer, because in being converted, we are likewise communicating with and being taught by God Himself. Magically this figures into purposes involving enlightenment, knowledge, and conversion to the faith.

The Sorrowful Mysteries (Mysteria Dolorosa)
In the First Sorrowful Mystery, the **Agony in the Garden**, we see a higher analogue of the Fourth Joyous, because obedience to Divine Law takes its logical conclusion in submission to the Divine Will. This submission, in order to be a true act of submission, must be given out of trust and pious love. It also goes further than this, because to bring oneself to obey, it requires a purgation of the urge to disobey. In fact, all the Sorrowful Mysteries are purgative in character, as they all involve purging something. From a magical perspective, this can be associated with purposes involving submission, restraint, or resolve.

The Second Sorrowful Mystery, the **Scourging at the Pillar**, has the spiritual fruit of gaining control over one's lower and carnal nature. This ties it in with purposes where self-control is needed in matters of the flesh, which can include prayers for your teenage son not to be controlled by his raging hormones!

The Third Sorrowful Mystery, the **Crowning with Thorns**, has for its fruit the gaining of control over one's thoughts and emotions. This Mystery is especially handy when striving not only to remove pride and unwanted thoughts/emotions from one's psyche, but also in the pursuit of peace, be it peace within oneself or peace within a community. I say this because its focus is the remove (or at least control) that which would cause contention, and thus has a side effect of creating an environment conducive to peaceful relations.

The Fourth Sorrowful Mystery, the **Carrying of the Cross**, has for its object perseverance exemplified by Our Lord patiently carrying the Cross. From this Mystery we learn patience (the root word of which is the Latin *pati*, "to suffer") and gain the courage to persevere, even in times of the most heinous persecution and suffering. This can be applied to purposes involving suffering, endurance, patience, silence (as Our Lord didn't complain as he carried the Cross), and to some degree strength and empowerment through the ability to persevere.

The Fifth Sorrowful Mystery, the **Crucifixion**, teaches us to die unto ourselves, and the mutual forgiveness both of those we have offended and those who have offended us. This brings into play intentions of penance, desensitization to the physical condition (thus a higher analogue of the Third Joyous Mystery), working through sorrow, and the strength to overcome crises and forgive those who caused them.

The Glorious Mysteries (Mysteria Gloriosa)

As we progress from the Joyful to the Sorrowful Mysteries, there's a shift of mood from one of beginning and initiation, to one of pain and purgation. As we progress from the Sorrowful and into the Glorious Mysteries, we see the mood change from one of suffering and purgation and into one of happiness, joy, and completion.

This transition of mood is very much brought forth in the First Glorious Mystery, the **Resurrection**, in which the Son has come back from the dead and is now the Sun of our spiritual lives. St. Paul tells us that if the Resurrection didn't happen, then our faith is all nothing but make-believe nonsense (1 Corinthians 15:14), and so this Mystery's fruit is the strengthening and continued firmness of that faith. This Mystery lends itself well to applications involving the defense of one's faith, the protection of loved ones from being influenced by those want them to abandon their faith, and for an increased knowledge and love of Christ and the economy of salvation.

The process of fulfillment continues in the Second Glorious Mystery, the **Ascension of Jesus**. Here we have the completion of the Third Joyous, in which not only are we indifferent and have we died to the physical world, but we have now shown our mastery over it to such a point that we've transcended it. This Mystery can teach us that if we wish to enter our spiritual home, we must first conquer and transcend the temptations, influences, and limitations of this one. It is only after we've conquered that we enter into the habitations of the Church Triumphant.

After Jesus ascended into Heaven, ten days later he sent the Holy Ghost to come down upon the Blessed Mother and the Apostles. This, the Third Glorious Mystery, the **Descent of the Holy Ghost**, is a completion of the Fifth Joyous because, as the Doctors and Priests were confounded by the prepubescent Christ, we now see the adult, conquering, and reigning Christ send down the Holy Ghost to lead us into all truth. This Mystery applies to the intentions of truth-finding, of gaining profound knowledge, and of seeking an amplification of the gifts of the Holy Ghost, which is the spiritual fruit of this Mystery.

For another fifteen years, the Blessed Mother is said to have remained upon this earth, until such time that God saw fit to call for her. Here, as God had done with Enoch, Moses, and Elijah, He chose to bring her body and soul directly into Heaven, which we call the **Assumption**. The spiritual fruit of this Mystery is a happy death, and this brings the sense of rest after labor, completion of work, and the peace of a well-earned reward. This Mystery can therefore be applied to works involving retirement, prayers for the souls in Purgatory, or anything else involving the peace and reward that should come after a prolonged period of hard work and right living.

This whole process comes to completion in the fifteenth and last Mystery, the **Coronation of Mary**. Here we have the final completion of a cycle that began with a fifteen-year old girl consenting to bear God Himself in her womb, and now she receives the full reward of her answer: "Behold the handmaid of the Lord! Be it done to me according to thy word!" In the Forty-Eighth chapter of St. Louis' book, he tells us that there's also a crown that awaits us in heaven should we persevere in the good fight, and the spiritual fruit is the reception of this crown. This can apply to all works of spiritual unity, spiritual reward, and completion, much as the Assumption would apply to these things on the physical level.

Observant readers may notice that I've intentionally excluded the "Luminous Mysteries" created by Pope John Paul II in 2002 and described in his encyclical *Rosarium Virginis Mariae*. These extra Mysteries were added as an option, and those who wish to use that option are welcome to do so. I prefer to keep to the traditional Rosary because brings to the table a balance between prayer, spiritual fruit, and spiritual life that's been perfected over centuries. Without prejudice to the newer form, I just happen to believe that "If it ain't broke, don't fix it."

The Proper Use of the Rosary
Even though the individual Mysteries may have applications to particular magical purposes, it is best that we not pick and choose each Mystery for its relevance to our operations. Rather, it's better that we pray the entire Rosary as directed by the Church, praying those Mysteries on the days in which they are associated: Joyful on Monday and Thursday, Sorrowful on Tuesday and Friday, and Glorious on Wednesday and Saturday. Sundays are divided amongst the three sets: Joyful between Advent and Ash Wednesday, Sorrowful between Ash Wednesday and Easter, and Glorious between Easter and Advent.

To better understand this, perhaps it would benefit us to think of the Rosary as the visible spectrum of light, and the Mysteries as colors in that spectrum. Now as to color, Birren argues that the skin must contain cells which pick out the colors the body needs from white light and applies it to its needs (*Color Psychology*, p. 132). Arguing from this logic, the Entire Rosary would be as a ray of sunlight, from which our operations will pick out the appropriate "colors" and apply them to our lives. Thus we get the benefit not only of the one or two Mysteries that most apply, but rather of all the Mysteries, which will help keep us in balance and maybe even help avoid the side-effects which sometimes come with magical operations.

Rosary Novenae
Because the Rosary is so effective, many people have thoroughly integrated it into all parts of their devotional lives. A well-known part of this devotional life is the Novena, or nine-day prayer made for special requests and petitions.

To use the Rosary in a Novena is simple, in that all you need do is set up your candles on your mensa and then pray the Rosary for nine days straight.

Perhaps the longest Rosary novena is the one mentioned earlier, that of Our Lady of Pompeii; it was allegedly given by Our Lady in 1884 and takes 54 days. For the first twenty-seven days, you meditate on the Mysteries appropriate to each day and pray in petition. On the last twenty-seven days, you meditate on the Mysteries in thanksgiving.

Rosary novenas and prayerbooks are readily available on the internet, and they offer a wealth of examples you can use. There's a lot out there, including prayers you may never even have thought existed, so feel free to explore!

There is also a text file on the internet composed by Cindy Smith titles "Rosaries of All Kinds," which gives a detailed look at all the different kinds of Rosaries and Saint Chaplets available. This file can be found at: http://www.textfiles.com/occult/CHRISTIAN/rosary.txt

This text file, which I recommend to anyone interested in the many other forms which the Rosary has taken over the centuries, should also provide a springboard to those who wish to explore and meditate upon how to expand the Rosary's devotional and magical implications.

VI. PRACTICAL CANDLE OPERATIONS

We've examined the different aspects which a Catholic mage can incorporate into his use of candle burning magic. Now, at this point, we provide a number of candle-based operations to give the reader ideas and insight by way of example.

This chapter will then be divided into four sections, each one corresponding to the four major categories of magical purposes: Love, Money, Health, and Protection.

Love
Because of the types of operations which appear in other books, I would like to state here that the operations given under this category will have nothing to do with the manipulation of another person's perceptions or of going out to find a one-night stand. Rather, these are of a more general nature, involving the finding and preservation of love especially as expressed in the Sacrament of Matrimony.

1. To Find a Suitable Mate:
Let's face it: many of us are in situations where we're lonely and just not able to find that right person. In fact we may be convinced that right person doesn't exist in our local area. The internet's proven itself an equally dismal place to search, since the male/female distribution isn't the greatest. So in this situation, what do you do?

Materials:
Red male or female figure candle
Vase of Roses (as many as you want, but at least six)
Image or Statue of St. Therese, to the right of figure candle.
Image of Holy Family, to the left of the figure candle.
Medal of St. Therese

This ritual should ideally be performed on a Friday, and calls upon both the Holy Family and St. Therese for help.

1. Before beginning the rite, you should spend some time in meditation before the mensa. Light the altar candles and proceed to meditate on your goal, visualizing yourself as having found you perfect mate and spending time with her, going to a movie or out to dinner, planning a marriage, or whatever. The important thing is to keep it chaste and keep it simple. You may also want to perform the "Meditation on the Divine Presence" (found in Chapter Seven of my *The Magic of Catholicism*) at this space as well.

2. After your meditation, arise and proceed to the mensa, and state your Declaration of Intent:
I do this that I may find the perfect mate. Holy Family, bring this perfect person to me now. St. Therese, send down your roses from heaven that the spouse of my dreams shall soon be in mine arms!

3. Take the red figure candle into your left hand and hold your right hand over it, saying:
This candle is my perfect mate, lover, and spouse, whoever and wherever she (he) may be. May almighty God +bless and +sanctify this candle, imbuing it with the dew of heavenly sweetness, that by this work which I am about to perform, the burning of this candle shall call to her (him) and swiftly bring her (him) into my arms.

Sprinkle the candle three times with holy water.

4. Light the candle, saying:
As I light this red candle, so does it become a burning flame within the heart of my perfect mate, calling her (him) to me and drawing her (him) into my arms.

5. Looking at the image of the Holy Family, recite prayer number 7 from Appendix A:
**O Jesus, lover of the young, the dearest Friend I have, in all confidence I open my heart to You to beg Your light and assistance in the important task of planning my future. Give me the light of Your grace, that I may decide wisely concerning the person who is to be my partner through life. Dearest Jesus, send me such a one whom in Your divine wisdom You judge best suited to be united with me in marriage. May her/his character reflect some of the traits of Your own Sacred Heart. May s/he be upright, loyal, pure, sincere and noble, so that with united efforts and with pure and unselfish love we both may strive to perfect ourselves in soul and body, as well as the children it may please You to entrust to our care. Bless our friendship before marriage, that sin may have no part in it. May our mutual love bind us so closely, that our future home may ever be most like Your own at Nazareth.
O Mary Immaculate, sweet Mother of the young, to your special care I entrust the decision I am to make as to my future wife/husband. You are my guiding Star! Direct me to the person with whom I can best cooperate in doing God's Holy Will, with whom I can live in peace, love and harmony in this life, and attain to eternal joys in the next. Amen.**

6. Pick up the roses and place them next to the image of St. Therese, if they are not there already. Say:

St. Therese, Little Flower of the Child Jesus, who said you would send down roses from Heaven to those who call upon you. Receive this offering of roses now, and intercede alongside the Holy Family on my behalf, bringing to me the one with whom I am to properly share my life and my love. I am tired of (going to bars, searching the internet, being set up with friends of friends, etc., as applies to your personal situation), and now seek only to find the one with whom my life is to be shared. Intercede for me, Little Flower, that this person shall come to me, and be known to me, and be in my arms quickly. Through Christ our Lord. Amen.

7. Pick up the medal and place it around your neck, saying: **As I place this medal around my neck, so too do I place my confidence in the intercession of the Little Flower of the Child Jesus, that she shall steer me correctly to my perfect love. Amen.**

8. You should now sit, stand, or kneel (whichever is your usual custom) and pray five decades of the Rosary, using the Mysteries proper to that day and meditating on your petition. Offer this Rosary to the Holy Family for their assistance; next to the Mass, the Rosary is the sweetest and most powerful offering that can possibly be made.

9. When you are finished, say a prayer of Thanks to almighty God and the Saints for having assisted you in this endeavor. Now, every day for the next nine days, you will repeat this entire operation, thus making it a novena. The only exception to this is that you will not repeat the blessing and sprinkling of the candle in step 3.

10. While you perform this novena and even afterward, wear the medal around your neck and keep the roses watered and as well cared-for as your ability will allow.

These roses are an offering, and therefore should not be allowed to rot and wither away before their time. When the ritual is finished, go to the nearest shrine of St. Therese and place them as close as possible to her image, relic, or side altar, thus completing the offering.

2. To Keep or Restore Peace in a Marriage

I like to think that we're all realists, and reality is even the best marriages have their snags where communication just isn't happening or the partners are at each other's throat. When this occurs, you can work this operation in order to create an atmosphere where the problem can be brought into the open and dealt with in a more constructive manner.

This rite calls upon the intercession of Blessed Luigi and Maria Beltrame Quattrocchi, who were beatified by Pope John Paul II in 2002 and are looked upon as the patrons of the married estate.

It should be noted from the onset, however, that this operation will only work if both spouses honestly and truly want the marriage to heal. There are times where one or the other spouse is causing problems and trying to force a break-up, instead of being a responsible adult and openly communicating with his or her partner. In cases like these, there's no magical operation that'll fix the situation, and in the long run it may be better for both parties to let the marriage die.

Materials:
White 7-Day Candle
Image of Blessed Luigi and Maria Quattrocchi
Picture of wife (to left of candle)
Picture of husband (to right of candle)
Piece of paper

1. In front of your mensa, sit in meditation upon your goal, that the problems in your (or your friend's or client's) marriage may be solved. Imagine the two of them sitting in a lavender room with white lace curtains, a cool gentle breeze coming through the window and cooling them off, while they sit and gently discuss the issues at hand. Having come to a working resolution, imagine them holding one another in their arms, and giving each other a kiss, signifying that love has once again returned and the problem is overcome. Finally, a brilliant white light, the light of God's blessing and Providence, comes in through the window and envelops the couple as they stand in loving embrace.

2. Arise and approach the mensa. Make your Declaration of Intent in your own words, an example of which follows:
I do this because the marriage of N. and N.N. has come to trouble. Blessed Luigi and Maria Quattrocchi, intercede on behalf of my petitions before the Father, that this marriage shall become fresh, loving, and free of these adversities as you both loved one another.

Now place the pictures of husband and wife on top of one another. Whether wife-over-husband or husband-over-wife doesn't matter, just do what feels right.

3. On the paper in front of you, write:
N. and N.N. have conquered the obstacles to a happy marriage.

and place this paper on the mensa, on top of the pictures.

4. Picking up the white 7-Day candle in your left hand, bless it with the right, saying:
+Bless, O Lord of Hosts, this candle which we in thy name +bless, that its oily wax shall symbolize the grease

and filth of the obstacles keeping peace from returning to the marriage of N. and N.N., and so as it is burned away by this purifying flame which is the light of thy Son, so too shall all obstacles be burned away from the marriage of N. and N.N. Through Christ our Lord. Amen.

And sprinkle the candle three times with holy water, saying nothing. Place the candle on top of the paper and the pictures and light it.

5. Fixating on the flame of the candle, say this prayer:
Blessed Luigi and Maria Quattrocchi, come to my aid and intercede on behalf of my petitions before the Father! Help restore peace and harmony to this troubled marriage between N. and N.N., and may they again remember the meaning and purpose of this holy Sacrament through which their souls are both entwined. Bring them peace, bring them harmony, bring them comfort, and help them join together to crush any obstacles in the way to their happy union. Through Jesus Christ our Lord, who with the Father lives and reigns in the unity of the Holy Ghost, God, forever and ever. Amen.

6. Now sit back and meditate again on your objective, visualizing as you did in step 1. If possible, you may also want to say a Rosary here for your intentions.

7. Say this prayer of thanks:
Blessed Luigi and Maria Quattrocchi, I give you thanks for your intercession, that you have helped to heal the marriage of N. and N.N. Amen.

8. You are finished for this night. Now leave the candle burning until it burns out on its own, and for each day that it burns, repeat steps 5 to 8 inclusive.

3. To Construct a Love Charm

Common wisdom has it that the best charm for attracting love is within yourself: work on yourself, improve yourself, and make yourself inwardly attractive, and people will be more drawn to you; this is similar to the late-nineteenth century concept of the "Law of Attraction." There is a great deal of truth in this, but sometimes we need a little extra help to point us in the right direction.

Sometimes all we need is something to make us feel more attractive: a shave, a change in wardrobe, just bathing more often, or even going to a new location where you can meet available people. Other times we might just be like Linus and need a "security blanket," which in this case would be a piece of jewelry that helps us to feel more confident and beautiful (which is the only non-superstitious way to explain how most love talismans work). And other times, we just need divine guidance outright.

For these times, I propose the consecration and use of a love charm which can be worn around the neck or placed in the pocket while going out. This won't help you to go out to a bar and "get laid," but is instead intended to help you keep your focus on the divine guidance as to how you yourself can become and feel more attractive, and in response others will find themselves more attracted to you. While there's no miracle that will do this overnight, the idea here is to help accelerate the process.

Materials:
Love charm (described in step 1)
Red 7/8" straight candle

Green 7/8" straight candle
Optional: Holy Water or Rose oil mixed with cinnamon.

1. Procure the love charm itself, which can be anything from a charm on a bracelet or necklace, a copper nugget with the symbol of Venus etched upon it, or a piece of jewelry that you feel has an especial connection with attraction and attractiveness.

2. Place the red and green candles side-by-side, upon the center of your mensa. The green candle should be on the left, the red on the right. Place the charm in front of the candles.

3. Make your Declaration of Intent, which may be something like the following:
I perform this work that this talisman of love may be consecrated, thus shall love and romance be brought into the life of N. Amen.

4. Now we begin the rite of blessing the talisman, saying:
Our help is in the name of the Lord.

Then either you or an assistant respond:
Who made the heaven and the earth.

You say:
The Lord be with you.

Then either you or an assistant respond:
And with your spirit.

Finally, you say **Let us pray**, and then place left hand on the mensa, right hand over the talisman, while saying the prayer of blessing:
Most benign and almighty God, whose name is called

Adonai Sabaoth when in the Sphere of Nesah: we ask Thee vouchsafe to look upon the humbleness of this creature of metal (*or* wood, *or* leather, *or* papyrus, *or* paper, *or whatever*), and impart to it the bles+sing of Thy divine power, that, in keeping with the spirit of the sigils and characters inscribed upon its surface, it may attract to the operator, or towards whomever carrieth or may possess this amulet, great love, physical as well as spiritual, and the spirit of mental as well as physical attraction. Through our Lord Jesus Christ, Thy Son, who liveth and reigneth with Thee in the unity of the Holy Ghost, God, forever and ever.

After the prayer is concluded, either you or an assistant finalize the blessing by saying: **Amen.**

5. Now that the blessing has been given, you have the option of sprinkling it with holy water thrice in the form of a cross (in silence), or you may anoint it with a mixture of rose and cinnamon oil, also in the form of a cross, while saying:
By this holy anointing, and His most loving mercy, may the almighty Lord impart to this amulet the power of amorous attraction.

Here you anoint the amulet, saying:
In the name of the Father, and of the +Son, and of the Holy Ghost. Amen.

4. To Get Someone to Think About You
In a relationship, there may be times when you're separated from your beloved over a great distance or for a period of time, and you may have no way of getting in touch to see how they're doing or even say "I love you." This can be painful and even agonizing, so here's something to send them a message and get them to contact you.

The general principle of this rite rests in working with guardian angels as intermediaries between you and your beloved. It's been said that if you cannot reach another person or are having a problem with a person, you should ask your guardian angel to talk it over with his or her guardian angel, and then things will start to move in a more positive direction.

Of course, the drawback is that if you're dealing with someone who's dense as a ton of bricks, then neither this nor any other operation will be successful; since magic is an art of dealing with subtle energies, those who have no receptivity or sensitivity to energy will simply not be effected one way or the other.

Materials:
One red candle (7/8" straight or figure candle).
Usual mensa candles (7/8" straight, 2 white and 1 red).
Piece of Paper.
Pen with either red or black ink.
Mixture of rose and rosemary oil.

1. Place your red figure candle in the center of the mensa, with the piece of paper in front of it; do not light the candle. Your mensa candles should be in the usual place.

2. With hands joined upon the mensa, make your Declaration of Intent, which could be like this:
I do this that I may enjoy the thoughts of N., that N. shall think about me pleasantly and contact me presently.

3. Anoint the red candle with the oil mixture, by whatever method you prefer. On the piece of paper, write the name of the person you wish to think about you. Write nine times:

N., think about me and come to me.

4. After writing this out, anoint the paper with a mixture of rose and rosemary oil in the form of a cross, and then fold it into quarters. Place the paper underneath the red candle.

5. Light the red candle, praying as you do so:
Almighty God, unto whom all secrets are known and by whom the hearts of the human race are bestirred. Send forth thine Holy Spirit and transmit thy power into this my work. By the intercession of St. Gabriel, whom thou sent as a messenger to Daniel and to the Blessed Virgin Mary; by the intercession of St. Martha, one of whose charges is to keep us on our lover's minds; and by the actions of mine and N.'s guardian angels, I seek that the heart of N. be such bestirred, that N. shall keep me in his/her thoughts, and that N. shall contact me at the first possible opportunity. Through our Lord Jesus Christ thy Son, who liveth and reigneth in the unity of the same Holy Ghost, God, world without end. Amen.

6. Once you finish this prayer, say the following address to Sts. Gabriel and St. Martha:
O glorious St. Gabriel, thou who wast chosen by Almighty God to bring messages to the sons and daughters of men, so too do I call upon thee to bring N. the tidings of my love. O wondrous St. Martha, sister of Lazarus who was called back from death by our Lord. It is said that one of your provinces is the closeness between lovers. Thus I seek thee, thus I ask thee, thus I come before thee to draw N. closer to me. Keep me in his/her thoughts, keep me in his/her dreams, keep me in his/her fantasies, that he/she shall come to me or call me at the first possible opportunity. Through Christ our Lord. Amen.

And finally, the Guardian Angel prayer:
Angel of God, my guardian dear, to whom his love commits me here; ever this day (night) be at my side, to light and guard, to rule and guide.

If you know your guardian Angel's name, you may say "**Angel N**" in the above prayer, in place of "Angel of God."

7. Keeping your hands joined, continue the prayer thus:
O holy Guardian Angel, deputed from birth to guide and to protect me to the end of my years: guide me, advocate for me, and present my case for me now. Go, I ask you, to the guardian Angel of N., and persuade him to place my countenance in N.'s thoughts, my voice in N.'s dreams, and my touch in N.'s fantasies. Persuade him so to make my image, my voice, and my touch so compellingly real and palpable to N, that N. shall come to me straightaway, or at the first possible opportunity. I seek this through the power of our Lord Jesus Christ, who with the Father liveth and reigneth in the unity of the Holy Ghost, God, world without end. Amen.

8. Remain standing for a few minutes, imagining your loved one thinking, dreaming, and fantasizing about you. Then imagine him or her calling you and getting back in touch with you.

When the time comes that you feel is right – and it's important not to rush this step – inhale, while separating your hands and holding them over the candle. As you exhale, imagine the energy from these visualizations going out from the palms of your hands and into the candle, giving the ritual fuel to draw your beloved back to you.

9. When you are finished, leave the candle burning, and say a prayer of thanksgiving to Almighty God, to Sts. Gabriel

and Martha, and to your Guardian Angel for the work they have accomplished on your behalf. Amen.

Money
1. To gain money in a hurry
Is it just me, or do we all have those times when we need to stretch to pay the bills? Of course, you can go to those check-cashing places for a "fast payday loan," but then you'll just get caught up in a vicious web of debt that's nigh impossible to escape. You can take up a second job, but then you'll have no time for the kids and it'll be up to three weeks before you see your first paycheck! You need the money now, so here's a suggestion:

Materials:
1 Green light bulb
1 Green 7-day candle
1 Brown 7-day candle
2 White 7-day candles
2 Green votive glass candle-holders
14 tealights
Pen with Green Ink
Piece of unlined paper
Piece of Paper Currency ($1, $5, $10, or $20 bill)

1. This rite assumes a room where your materials will be undisturbed for the duration of the working, no matter what else is done in that room. So start by unscrewing whatever light bulb is currently in use, and replace it with the green bulb. This bulb is to be kept lit constantly for the duration of the ritual.

2. The two white 7-Day candles will be your mensa candles for this operation, so bless them and set them up accordingly.

3. Place the money on the center of the mensa, and on the piece of paper write nine times: **Much money comes quickly to N.**, where "N." is your name. Place this on top of the currency.

4. Place the Brown and Green 7-day candles on top of the paper, with the brown to the left and the green to the right. The green candle represents the energy of wealth that you wish to manifest, and the brown candle represents the channel of speedy manifestation for that energy. Bear this in mind as you proceed.

5. Place the votive glasses in front of the 7-day candles, with a tea light in each.

6. Make your Declaration of Intent:
I do this because I need money, in the amount of x inside the next y days. Almighty God, through your Angels and through your Saints I draw nigh that you will grant this to me. In this statement, x is the amount of money you need, and y is the amount of time in which you need it.

7. Light your mensa candles, saying nothing as you do so, but thinking about the money you need. Visualize yourself already having it and happily holding it in your hands. Picture yourself paying your bills, getting out of debt, and investing and growing your future.

8. Now light the Green and Brown 7-day candles, in that order, saying:

At the green: **From spiritual force**.
At the brown: **Unto physical form be manifest**.

9. Light the tea lights, also from right to left, in silence. Then, bowing with hands joined upon the mensa, say this prayer:
Almighty Eternal God, whose name is El when thou presidest over the Sphere of Hesed: by the intercession of St. Joseph, the Foster-Father of thy Son our Lord and patron of workers, and by the rising up of Sadkiel, the Archangel of the Hesedic Shpere, I call unto thee, I draw nigh unto thee, and I invoke thee. I invoke thee into this my work that thou wilt give ear unto my plea, and that by sending forth thy light and thy grace this work shall be successful. Help me, O Lord, to gain x amount of dollars in y day's time, that my physical needs and those of my loved ones shall be met, and that we shall thus be able to turn our whole minds, hearts, and souls to the contemplation of thy glory. Through our same Lord, Jesus Christ, thy Son, who liveth and reigneth with thee in the unity of the Holy Ghost, God, forever and ever. Amen.

10. Afterwards, go about your daily business while leaving the candles to burn. Each day, you will replace the tea lights with fresh ones, light them, and say the above prayer; the money you seek should be in your hands by the end of the ritual.

<u>2. To Bring Money into a Business Venture</u>
Okay, so you've shelled out for all necessary and legal and licensing requirements, you've got the building or office space, and you've got the product, whatever that may be. It's your first day on the job, and you want customers! Here's a short and simple operation to be carried out daily, to help draw customers (and revenue) into your sphere of availability.

This rite invokes the Holy Family and especially the Infant Jesus of Prague. In traditional Benedicaria practice, it is believed that to the Infant of Prague can ensure a steady flow of income into the home. We elaborate on this, and also encourage the practitioner to place a statue or image of the Infant facing the door of his place of business.

Materials:
1 Virgin Mary 7-day Candle (in any of her titles)
1 St. Joseph 7-day Candle
1 Infant Jesus of Prague 7-day Candle
1 Piece of Unlined Paper
1 Pen with Green Ink

1. As above, and as in all rites, we assume that your mensa will be set up in a place where it won't be disturbed for the entire time of the operation.

2. The mensa is to be set up as follows: on the left, far corner shall be placed the candle of the Virgin Mary; on the right, far corner the candle of St. Joseph; and in the center, front shall be placed the candle of the Infant Jesus. Under the "Jesus Candle" you place the piece of paper, with the saying **I want money to come to my business** written on it nine times.

3. Light the "Mary Candle," then recite Prayer #8 from Appendix A:
O Mother of Perpetual Help! Grant that I may ever invoke your most powerful name, which is the safeguard of the living and the salvation of the dying. O purest Mary! O sweetest Mary! Let your name henceforth be ever on my lips. Delay not, O Blessed Lady, to succor me whenever I call on you. In all my temptations, in all my needs, I will never cease to call on you ever repeating your sacred name. Mary, Mary. Oh,

what a consolation, what sweetness, what confidence, what emotion fills my soul when I utter your sacred name, or even only think of you! I thank the Lord for having given you, for my good, so sweet, so powerful, so lovely a name. But I will not be content with merely uttering your name. Let my love for you prompt me ever to hail you Mother of Perpetual Help. Mother of Perpetual Help, pray for me and grant me the favor I confidently ask of you, that my business shall generate enough money to pay my bills, my expenses, and all the needs of survival, that through thee I may glorify thy Son more and more.

4. From this, we light the "Joseph Candle," while praying the oration for Success in Work, which is #13 from Appendix A:
Glorious St. Joseph, model of all those who are devoted to labor, obtain for me the grace to work conscientiously, putting the call of duty above my many sins; to work with thankfulness and joy, considering it an honor to employ and develop, by means of labor, the gifts received from God; to work with order, peace, prudence and patience, never surrendering to weariness or difficulties; to work, above all, with purity of intention, and with detachment from self, having always death before my eyes and the account which I must render of time lost, of talents wasted, of good omitted, of vain complacency in success so fatal to the work of God. All for Jesus, all for Mary, all after thy example, O Patriarch Joseph. Such shall be my motto in life and death. Amen.

Follow with this prayer:
Glorious St. Joseph, pray for me and grant me the favor I confidently ask of you, that my business shall generate enough money to pay my bills, my expenses, and all the

needs of survival, that through thee I may glorify Our Lord more and more.

5. Finally, we come to the "Jesus Candle," which we light while reciting the Novena to the Infant Jesus of Prague, which is #2 from Appendix A:
O Jesus, who hast said, "Ask and you shall receive, seek and you shall find, knock and it shall be opened to you," through the intercession of Mary, Thy most holy Mother, I knock, I seek, I ask that my prayer be granted.

Here mention your request:
Holy Infant of Prague, come to me and grant me the favor I confidently ask of you, that my business shall generate enough money to pay my bills, my expenses, and all the needs of survival, that I may humbly glorify Thee more and more.

Continue the Novena prayer:
O Jesus, who hast said, "All that you ask of the Father in My Name, He will grant you," through the intercession of Mary, Thy most holy Mother, I humbly and urgently ask Thy Father in Thy Name that my prayer be granted.

Again mention your request:
Holy Infant of Prague, come to me and grant me the favor I confidently ask of you, that my business shall generate enough money to pay my bills, my expenses, and all the needs of survival, that I may humbly glorify Thee more and more.

Continue the Novena prayer:
O Jesus, who hast said, "Heaven and earth shall pass away, but My word shall not pass," through the

intercession of Mary, Thy most holy Mother, I feel confident that my prayer will be granted.

Again mention your request:
Holy Infant of Prague, come to me and grant me the favor I confidently ask of you, that my business shall generate enough money to pay my bills, my expenses, and all the needs of survival, that I may humbly glorify Thee more and more.

6. Meditate in front of the candles, contemplating the Holy Family and how they have helped you in your life; know now that they are helping you now, and will continue to do so. You wish to follow their example, so let them know that by reciting Prayer #6 from Appendix A:
Lord Jesus Christ, who, being made subject to Mary and Joseph, didst consecrate domestic life by Thine ineffable virtues; grant that we, with the assistance of both, may be taught by the example of Thy Holy Family and may attain to its everlasting fellowship. Who livest and reignest forever. Amen.

7. Now give thanks to the Holy Family for their assistance, in your own words, and say it devoutly and sincerely. The Holy Family love and will help you as a result of that love. It's only right love them back and freely express that love, the same way you would express love for your own family.

8. This ends the first day. Now for each day that the candles burn, sit and meditate in front of them, and say the prayers indicated throughout the text of this rite. Once the candles burn down, replace them and begin the rite over again, making this a daily devotion.

3. Finding a New Job

Back in the 90's, nobody had problems finding a job. You could grab something and if you didn't like it, you'd have another job within an hour's time. It's not like that anymore, and no matter how much recovery we might see in the stock markets, a lot of people still don't have jobs and the market's still tough.

Sometimes, we just need a little lift.

The following exercise is aimed at doing just that: finding new employment quickly. It may not be the best-paying job or a job with the most dignity, but you'll find something to support yourself and your family, which can give you a springboard to move on to something better before long.

Materials:
1 Yellow or (preferably) St. Joseph 7-day Candle
1 Blue or (preferably) Virgin Mary 7-day Candle
28 Tea lights or Votive Candles
2 Yellow Votive Candleholders
2 Blue Votive Candleholders
Altar Candles (see Chapter 4, p. 104)
1 Green Lightbulb.
Rosary

1. Light the lightbulb, which should be the only light in the room.

2. On your mensa, place the Altar Candles first (Chapter IV, figure 4-1). Then place the Virgin Mary and St Joseph Candles in the center, with Mary on the left and Joseph on the right. Finally, place the blue Votive holders in front of Mary and the Yellow ones in front of Joseph. Place tea lights or Votive candles in these.

3. For a few seconds, quietly meditate on your purpose for doing this, and visualize yourself being employed and supporting yourself and your family. Your bills are paid, your rent or mortgage is current, and debt collectors are off your back. After formulating your intention, say out loud why you're doing this. Use your own words and keep it simple.

4. Light the Saint Joseph candle, saying:
St. Joseph, patron of workers and foster-father of Our Lord, intercede for me and help me to find a decent job.

5. Light the Blessed Mother candle, saying:
O Most Sorrowful and Immaculate Blessed Virgin Mary, Mother of God and Mother of the whole Church, interceded for me and help me find a decent job.

6. Light the Candles in the yellow holders, saying:
St. Joseph, pray for us, and intercede for us in the sight of Almighty God.

7. Light the candles in the blue holders, saying:
O Holy Mother of God, pray for us.
That we may be made worthy of the promises of Christ.

8. Take the Rosary in your hands, and assume the position you do when normally praying the Rosary (standing, sitting, or kneeling, as you find most comfortable and best for your mental concentration). Before starting, hold the Rosary in your hands and say:
May this offering of the Most Holy Rosary be found acceptable to Our Lady, and may she earnestly intercede on behalf of my petitions before the Father.

9. Pray the Rosary in the usual manner, meditating upon the Mysteries proper to that day of the week (see Chapter V). There is a technique with the Mysteries in which the Mystery is said in the middle of the Hail Mary, right after the name of Jesus. Here, we would insert the purpose of our working, such as:

"... *blessed is the fruit of thy womb, Jesus.*
Whose help I implore in finding suitable employment.
Holy Mary, Mother of God ..."

Finish out the Rosary saying the usual prayers in the usual manner.

10. After the Rosary is finished, end with this prayer: **O most Sorrowful and Immaculate Blessed Virgin Mary, Mother of God and Mother of men, thou who wast found worthy to carry God himself in thy womb, and thou who has crushed him who is at once the enemy of God and man in common under thy heel. Humbly do I, N., approach thee, through these Joyful (or Sorrowful, or Glorious) Mysteries of this thy Most Holy Rosary, asking that this offering may be acceptable to thee, and that thou wilt earnestly intercede on behalf of my petitions before the Father, namely that thou, with the help of St. Joseph, thy Spouse, and Jesus Christ, thy Son, will help me to find suitable employment. Through our same Lord Jesus Christ thy Son, who with the Father liveth and reigneth in the unity of the Holy Ghost, God, forever and ever. Amen.**

11. Finish this day by saying thanks for all the good you have received, and all the help you have received in finding a job. On all subsequent days, repeat step three to form your intention, and then repeat steps 6-11 every day.

Please realize that this ritual will not automatically make a job drop into your lap, as God helps them who help themselves. You must comb the papers, look for "Help Wanted" signs, search the internet high and low, and fill out your own job applications. However, this will be of great help (I've used it myself in the past!) finding employment when market is tight.

Health
<u>1. To Restore One's Health</u>
In the first place, Sacred Scripture tells us to honor the medical profession (Sirach 38:1), and we're not about to argue against Sacred Scripture. However, the Church also encourages us to seek out the intercession of the Saints during our trials in this life, especially when we need help in the more difficult cases.

Materials: Altar Candles
1 Yellow Taper Candle
1 St. Raphael Holy Card
1 St. Raphael Medal

1. Procure the St. Raphael Medal and have it blessed by your priest. If he asks why, do not lie to him. Tell him that it is for yourself or for a friend or family member (such as the case may actually be), and that you believe St. Raphael's intercession will help him or her to get better. If he wants more information, then feel free to show him this book and take whatever advice he gives you; please contact me on Facebook (name Agostino Taumaturgo) if you feel that advice is something I should hear about.

2. Once the medal is blessed, you may place it around your neck or the neck of the person for whom you're praying.

If possible, you may also set it down on your mensa when you pray, as a symbol of uniting your prayers with the medal.

3. Place the yellow candle in the center of your mensa, and light the Altar Candles in the usual fashion. Place the St. Raphael Holycard in front of the candle.

4. With hands joined, pray for St. Raphael's intercession, using Prayer #20 from Appendix A:
Glorious Archangel, Saint Raphael, great prince of the heavenly Court, you are illustrious for your gifts of wisdom and grace. You are a guide of those who journey by land, or sea, or air, consoler of the afflicted, and refuge of sinners. I beg you, assist me in all my needs and in all the sufferings of this life, as once you helped the young Tobias on his travels. Because you are the "medicine of God" I humbly pray you to heal the many infirmities of my soul and the ills that afflict my body. I especially ask of you the favor of healing N of the affliction the affects him/her, *(here name the affliction)*, **and the great grace of purity to prepare me to be the temple of the Holy Ghost. Amen.**

5. Now quietly meditate in front of the candle, and in your mind, imagine Raphael going up to the Seat of grace with your request and presenting it at the feet of God the Father. He then comes down, whether to you or to the person for whom you are praying, wraps his wings around him, and heals him or her. Don't just watch it, but feel it happening and believe that it's already happened. Remember what our Lord says in Mark 11:24: *"So I tell you, whatever you ask for in prayer, believe that you have received it, and it will be yours."*

6. Once finished, extinguish the candle and thank St. Raphael for helping you in this work. For nine days, keep lighting the candle, praying, and meditating.

2. For a Safe Childbirth

We all wish that our pregnancies, or those of our wives, would have a smooth and easy run from conception to delivery. Yet unfortunately, this isn't always the case.

In times like this, when there are complications with the pregnancy or the birth itself, or even just to ensure that all goes as it should, we look to the intercession of St. Gerard Majella and/or St. Anne to help us in these delicate times. Of course, the expectant mother should always be under the care of an obstetrician during the course of the pregnancy, and it is recommended that the procedure below be done both by the mother and by her husband as soon as they find out she's expecting.

Materials:
I White seven-day candle
2 White taper candles (other than the altar candles)
Images of St. Anne and of St. Gerard Majella
Holy Water

1. Set it up and light the altar candles in the usual manner, and place the white 7-day candle in the center of the mensa, with one of the white tapers to either side. Place the image of Saint Anne in front of the left-hand taper, and the image of St. Gerard in front of the right-hand taper.

2. Husband and wife should both make the sign of the Cross, if both are working together. In the case that either is working in solitude without the other present, the he or she makes the Sign of the Cross, and adapts everything below to the use of a single practitioner.

3. Operator makes the following Declaration of Intent:
Almighty God, truly hast Thou granted us a marvel in the form of this unborn child. And now, in this hour, we draw nigh to Thee, seeking that Thou wilt be favorable to our supplications, to ensure that this child shall be born healthily and without complications, that the world may wonder upon seeing this manifestation of Thine ineffible glory. Amen.

4. The mother (or father, if he's working alone) then lights the 7-day candle, praying as she does so:
As I light this candle on this day/night, so doth it represent my desire to see my child born into the world, healthy and without complications.

The father continues this prayer (or mother, if alone):
May Almighty God, Father, Son, and Holy Ghost, who has given us this wonderful child, assist us in bringing to term this pregnancy. For His wonder is seen in the eyes of every child, and to be as a little child is to enter into the kingdom of Heaven. Amen.

5. The mother (or father, if he is alone) lights the left-hand taper candle, and prays an adaptation of Prayer #26 from Appendix A:
Good St. Anne, you were especially favored by God to be the mother of the most holy Virgin Mary, the Mother of our Savior. By your power with your most pure daughter and with her divine Son, kindly obtain for us the grace and the favor we now seek, that this our child shall be allowed to be born into the world healthily and without complications. Please secure for us also forgiveness of our past sins, the strength to perform faithfully our daily duties and the help we need to persevere in the love of Jesus and Mary. Amen.

6. The father (or mother, if she is alone) lights the right-hand taper candle, and prays this adapted form of prayer #60 from Appendix A:
O Great Saint Gerard, beloved servant of Jesus Christ, perfect imitator of thy meek and humble Savior, and devoted Child of the Mother of God: enkindle within my heart one spark of that heavenly fire of charity which glowed in thine and made thee a seraph of love. O glorious Saint Gerard, because when falsely accused of crime, thou didst bear, like thy Divine Master, without murmur or complaint, the calumnies of wicked men, thou hast been raised up by God as Patron and Protector of expectant mothers. Preserve my wife from danger and from excessive pains accompanying childbirth, and shield the child which she now carries, that he or she may see the light of day and receive the lustral waters of baptism, through Jesus Christ our Lord. Amen.

7. Both parents should now kneel (the mother may stand or sit if her condition requires it), and say one Our Father, followed by nine Hail Marys, one for each month of pregnancy. When done, they should reflect in silence upon what they've requested, then rise and say in unison the following prayer of thanksgiving:
Almighty God, St. Anne, St. Gerard, we give thanks to all of you, for you have aided us in delivering this our child, healthily and without complications. Through Christ our Lord. Amen.

8. The father should make the sign of the Cross over the mother's womb (blessing his child), and then sprinkle the mother's womb with Holy Water. The taper candles are extinguished, the two then make the sign of the Cross, and the rite is concluded.

9. Every day while the 7-day candle continues to burn, the couple should repeat the following:
Declaration of Intent.
Light the taper candles, and repeat steps 5-8.

This operation can also be adapted as a Pro-Life devotion, by praying for an unborn infant that you know or for the unborn in general.

Protection
1. General Protection
We all have moments when we could use a little help, whether we need protection against evil spirits, our crabby neighbors, a mean-spirited supervisor, meddling in-laws, or any host of other evils, be they intentionally or unintentionally inflicted on us.

Were one to look through the various magical literature extant, there would be found numerous formulae for every kind of protection: against storms, against sorcery, and so on and so forth. These take the form of "hardening the aura," of making a circle of salt around oneself, of charging and wearing talismans, and any other thing that one can possibly imagine.

For myself, I'd say many of the operations found in these books are overly drawn-out, and some are just plain absurd.

However, there are many prayers and even Masses employed to invoke divine protection, and a number of Saints are patrons for protection against one or other kind of tribulation. So here's an all-around general procedure:

1. Look through the list of Saints given in Chapter III, and find one whose patronage includes your situation. For example, St. Christopher is for safe travel, St. Benedict for

protection against spiritual evil, and the Lorica of St. Patrick serves as an excellent protection against all manner of persons and conditions.

2. Get an image of that Saint and a white candle.

3. Light the candle and say a prayer to that Saint asking his or her intercession to protect you from whatever circumstance.

4. Thank the Saint for having interceded on your behalf.

5. Sprinkle yourself with Holy Water. In addition, you can wear a medal of the Saint in question, or carry a holycard in your purse or coat pocket.

Now, know that you are protected (repeat if you feel it necessary), and amend your life to live as a good Christian.

VII. IT'S OVER ALREADY?

As we come to the end of this book, I'd like to think we covered a lot of ground within its pages. We discussed Candle Magic within the context of orthodox Christianity, the various elements that go into it, and how it can be practiced. This book also has a more "hands-on" orientation than my other offerings, largely because Candle Magic is a form of "low magic," which is generally more concerned about the hands-on approach and less concerned with theology or philosophy.

Before we go our separate ways, I'd like to include some additional minor information that can help you along the way.

Reading Your Candles
Many books on the subject of Candle Magic say it's possible to "read" your candles and tell the effect your magic is having. I've found this to be true, and the trick is to watch the flames.

A strong, tall flame means a lot of energy is going into your purpose, or there are few obstacles keeping it from being fulfilled. It could also mean your objective is already under your nose.

A weak flame means there are obstacles that need to be overcome, or that very little energy is going into your goal. It may be unlikely that you're going to succeed this time.

If your candle keeps going out of its own accord: that means there's something really big in the way and your magic isn't going to work. Better to pack it up for the time being and take another look at the situation. Maybe you're not looking at it from the right angle, or maybe there's something hidden where you can't see it. It's equally possible that God may be keeping you from hurting yourself.

There are other ways to read if a flame burns to the left or the right, and so on, but I've not had much luck reading these other movements. I said before that I'm sticking with what I know, and what I've seen is that the strength, height, and heat of the flame are the most reliable indicators of how your magic is affecting the outside world.

Incense
Traditionally, books on Candle Magic often talk about incense. The books say that incense is something that stimulates the psychic centers and brings more energy into play, or they say that it calls good spirits or other such reasons that it's supposed to help you. Me, I say that most magicians work in closed rooms, so incense could mean a possible choking hazard, triggering of respiratory problems, and of course allergies for those who have them. This is where the individual needs to exercise discretion.

Incense comes in many forms, and you're free to use sticks, cones, or resin. My personal preference is resin, because it's typically of better quality than stick or cone incense and gives a stronger scent while it burns.

Resin incense is burned atop charcoal specially made for incenses (NOT barbecue charcoal!), and these charcoals can be found in church supply stores and various retailers online. One should know there are two types of charcoal: the regular kind that takes awhile to light, and there's the Greek charcoal that lights almost immediately. When you light the charcoal, it begins to spark and part of it will turn red as it heats up. Once the entire charcoal is red, it's ready for your incense.

The rules for incenses are many and varied, and different books give different names, meanings, and formulae. The best all-purpose incense is a combination of frankincense and myrrh, and church incenses in general are good for raising one's consciousness and setting a magical atmosphere. I'd recommend going to a church supply store and asking the clerk if you can smell some of the incenses to find out which you like best. (Some stores will let you and some won't. The only way to know is to go!)

For more specifically magical incense, it's possible to follow the same rules as for oils: find the incense that matches the Saint (rose for Mary, lily for Joseph, etc.) and use that either in place of or in addition to the frankincense and myrrh mixture. As with all things in Candle Magic, your only true limit is your imagination!

Disposing of Your Materials
Last but not least, there's the question of disposing of your materials. After every operation you're bound to have candle stubs, incense ashes, drips of wax, paper, and other items left behind. How do we dispose of them?

I once read a book that said you should take a paper bag and put your leftovers in it. Then cut an orange in half and put both halves in the bag. Finally, leave it on the front steps of the local church. (Herman Slater. *Magickal Formulary Spellbook*. 1987. Magickal Childe. New York.)

In my opinion, that's not the smartest idea. Rather, it's best either to bury the materials, burn them, or toss them in a river. In times of emergency, it's possible to put them in the regular trash, though I don't recommend it.

Those who live out in the country may have other options for their leftovers, too, and one could even take leftover wax from candles (used for the same purpose) and form that wax into new candles. Options do exist, though in the end I'd recommend putting your used materials in the river.

The End
This is it, we've now come to the last paragraph on our journey. As we part ways, know that I wish you well and every success in your endeavors, and that if you have any questions or just want to talk, look me up on Facebook under Agostino Taumaturgo. The Facebook page for my books is http://facebook.com/OccultCatholicism, feel free to stop by and hit the "like" button!

On a parting note, I would like to thank everybody who has been so helpful over these last several years: Vito and Peggy Quattrocchi, Rue Roselli, Ambrose Hawk, Chris Bilardi, Frater Abdiel, Frater Pneuma, and every last one of you reading a copy of this book.

Pax et Bonum, my friends!
Agostino Taumaturgo

APPENDIX A. PRAYERS TO THE SAINTS

This is the complete appendix from *The Things We Do: Ways of the Holy Benedetta*, containing 78 Prayers and Novenas to Jesus, Mary, and the Saints. It is only available in the paperback version of this book.

I. In Honor of Our Lord
1. Novena of Confidence to the Sacred Heart
O Lord Jesus Christ, to Thy most Sacred Heart, I confide this intention *(here mention your request)*. Only look upon me, then do what Thy Sacred Heart inspires. Let Thy Sacred Heart decide. I count on It. I trust in It. I throw myself on Its mercy. Lord Jesus! Thou wilt not fail me. Sacred Heart of Jesus, I trust in Thee. Sacred Heart of Jesus, I believe in Thy love for me. Sacred Heart of Jesus, Thy kingdom come.
O Sacred Heart of Jesus, I have asked Thee for many favors, but I earnestly implore this one. Take it, place it in Thy open, broken Heart; and when the Eternal Father looks upon it, covered with Thy Precious Blood, He will not refuse it. It will be no longer my prayer, but Thine, O Jesus, O Sacred Heart of Jesus, I place all my trust in Thee. Let me not be disappointed. Amen.

2. Novena in urgent Need to the Infant Jesus of Prague
To be said at the same time for nine consecutive hours, or for nine days.
O Jesus, who hast said, "Ask and you shall receive, seek and you shall find, knock and it shall be opened to you," through the intercession of Mary, Thy most holy Mother, I knock, I seek, I ask that my prayer be granted.
Mention your request
O Jesus, who hast said, "All that you ask of the Father in My Name, He will grant you," through the intercession of

Mary, Thy most holy Mother, I humbly and urgently ask Thy Father in Thy Name that my prayer be granted.
Mention your request
O Jesus, who hast said, "Heaven and earth shall pass away, but My word shall not pass," through the intercession of Mary, Thy most holy Mother, I feel confident that my prayer will be granted.
Mention your request

3. Prayer for the Sick
Dear Jesus, Divine Physician and Healer of the sick, we turn to you in this time of illness. O dearest comforter of the troubled, alleviate our worry and sorrow with your gentle love, and grant us the grace and strength to accept this burden. Dear God, we place our worries in your hands. We place our sick under your care and humbly ask that you restore your servant to health again. Above all, grant us the grace to acknowledge your will and know that whatever you do, you do for the love of us. Amen.

4. Make Me an Instrument of Your Peace
Lord, make me an instrument of Your peace. Where there is hatred, let me sow love; where there is injury, pardon; where there is doubt, faith; where there is despair, hope; where there is darkness, light; where there is sadness, joy. O, Divine Master, grant that I may not so much seek to be consoled as to console; to be understood as to understand; to be loved as to love; For it is in giving that we receive; it is in pardoning that we are pardoned; it is in dying that we are born again to eternal life.

5. Prayer before Study or Instructions
Incomprehensible Creator, the true Fountain of light and only Author of all knowledge: deign, we beseech Thee, to enlighten our understanding, and to remove from us all darkness of sin and ignorance. Thou, who makest eloquent

the tongues of those who lack utterance, direct our tongues, and pour on our lips the grace of thy blessing. Give us a diligent and obedient spirit, quickness of apprehension, capacity of retaining, and the powerful assistance of Thy holy grace; that what we hear or learn we may apply to Thy honor and the eternal salvation of our own souls. Amen.

II. To the Holy Family
6. Prayer in Honor of the Holy Family
LORD Jesus Christ, who, being made subject to Mary and Joseph, didst consecrate domestic life by Thine ineffable virtues; grant that we, with the assistance of both, may be taught by the example of Thy Holy Family and may attain to its everlasting fellowship. Who livest and reignest forever. Amen.

7. Prayer for a Good Husband or Wife
O Jesus, lover of the young, the dearest Friend I have, in all confidence I open my heart to You to beg Your light and assistance in the important task of planning my future. Give me the light of Your grace, that I may decide wisely concerning the person who is to be my partner through life. Dearest Jesus, send me such a one whom in Your divine wisdom You judge best suited to be united with me in marriage. May her/his character reflect some of the traits of Your own Sacred Heart. May s/he be upright, loyal, pure, sincere and noble, so that with united efforts and with pure and unselfish love we both may strive to perfect ourselves in soul and body, as well as the children it may please You to entrust to our care. Bless our friendship before marriage, that sin may have no part in it. May our mutual love bind us so closely, that our future home may ever be most like Your own at Nazareth.

O Mary Immaculate, sweet Mother of the young, to your special care I entrust the decision I am to make as to my future wife/husband. You are my guiding Star! Direct me to the person with whom I can best cooperate in doing God's Holy Will, with whom I can live in peace, love and harmony in this life, and attain to eternal joys in the next. Amen.

III. In Honor of Mary
8. To our Lady of Perpetual Help
O Mother of Perpetual Help! Grant that I may ever invoke your most powerful name, which is the safeguard of the living and the salvation of the dying. O purest Mary! O sweetest Mary! Let your name henceforth be ever on my lips. Delay not, O Blessed Lady, to succor me whenever I call on you. In all my temptations, in all my needs, I will never cease to call on you ever repeating your sacred name. Mary, Mary. Oh, what a consolation, what sweetness, what confidence, what emotion fills my soul when I utter your sacred name, or even only think of you! I thank the Lord for having given you, for my good, so sweet, so powerful, so lovely a name. But I will not be content with merely uttering your name. Let my love for you prompt me ever to hail you Mother of Perpetual Help.
Mother of Perpetual Help, pray for me and grant me the favor I confidently ask of you.
Hail Mary *(3 times)*.

9. Hail, Most Venerable Queen of Peace
Hail, most venerable Queen of Peace, most holy Mother of God, through the Sacred Heart of Jesus, thy Son, the Prince of Peace, procure for us the cessation of His anger, that so He may reign over us in peace. Remember, O most gracious Virgin Mary, that never was it known that anyone who sought thy intercession was left forsaken. Inspired with this confidence, I come unto thee. Despise not my petitions, O Mother of the Word, but graciously here and grant my prayer. O merciful, O kind, O sweet Virgin Mary. Amen.

10. Novena to the Blessed Virgin Mary

In the name of the Father, and of the Son, and of the Holy Ghost. *R.* Amen.

We fly to thy patronage, O holy Mother of God; despise not our petitions in our necessities, but deliver us always from all dangers, O glorious and blessed Virgin. *R.* Amen.

V. Hail, Mary, full of grace, the Lord is with thee.
R. Thou hast brought forth Him who made thee, and ever remain a virgin.

Memorare to Mary
Remember, O most gracious Virgin Mary, that never was it known that anyone who fled to thy protection, implored thy help, or sought thy intercession, was left unaided. Inspired with this confidence, we fly unto thee, O Virgin of virgins and Mother; to thee do we come; before thee we stand, sinful and sorrowful; O Mother of the Word Incarnate, despise not our petitions, but in thy mercy hear and answer us. *R.* Amen.

V. Blessed art thou among women.
R. And blessed is the fruit of thy womb.
O pure and immaculate and likewise blessed Virgin, who art the sinless mother of thy Son, the mighty Lord of the universe, thou who art inviolate and altogether holy, the hope of the hopeless and sinful, we sing thy praises. We bless thee as full of every grace, thou who borest the God-Man: we all bow low before thee; we invoke thee and implore thy aid. *R.* Amen.

Pause here to name your petitions.

V. O Mary, conceived without sin,
R. Pray for us who have recourse to thee.

Let us pray.
Holy Mary, succor the miserable, help the faint-hearted, comfort the sorrowful, pray for the people, plead for the clergy, intercede for all women consecrated to God; may all who keep thy holy commemoration feel now thy help and protection. Be ever ready to assist us when we pray, and bring back to us the answers to our prayers. Make it thy continual care to pray for the people of God, thou who, blessed by God, merited to bear the Redeemer of the world, who lives and reigns for ever and ever. R. Amen.

IV. In Honor of St. Joseph
11. To thee, O blessed Joseph
To thee, O blessed Joseph, do we come in our tribulation, and having implored the help of thy most holy Spouse, we confidently invoke thy patronage also. Through that charity which bound thee to the immaculate Virgin Mother of God and through the paternal love with which thou embraced the Child Jesus, we humbly beg thee to graciously regard the inheritance which Jesus Christ has purchased by his Blood, and with thy power and strength to aid us in our necessities.
O most watchful Guardian of the Holy Family, defend the chosen children of Jesus Christ; O most loving father, ward off from us every contagion of error and corrupting influence; O our most mighty protector, be propitious to us and from heaven assist us in our struggle with the power of darkness; and, as once thou rescued the Child Jesus from deadly peril, so now protect God's Holy Church from the snares of the enemy and from all adversity; shield, too, each one of us by thy constant protection, so that, supported by thy example and thy aid, we may be able to live piously, to die holy, and to obtain eternal happiness in heaven. Amen.

12. Remember, O Most Pure Spouse of the Virgin Mary

Remember, o most pure Spouse of the Virgin Mary, my sweet Protector Saint Joseph, never was it heard that anyone who implored thy help nor sought thy intercession was left unaided. Inspired by this confidence I come to thee and to thee do I fervently commend myself. Despise not my petitions, I beseech thee, foster Father of the Redeemer, but graciously hear them. Amen.

13. Prayer for Success in Work

Glorious St. Joseph, model of all those who are devoted to labor, obtain for me the grace to work conscientiously, putting the call of duty above my many sins; to work with thankfulness and joy, considering it an honor to employ and develop, by means of labor, the gifts received from God; to work with order, peace, prudence and patience, never surrendering to weariness or difficulties; to work, above all, with purity of intention, and with detachment from self, having always death before my eyes and the account which I must render of time lost, of talents wasted, of good omitted, of vain complacency in success so fatal to the work of God. All for Jesus, all for Mary, all after thy example, O Patriarch Joseph. Such shall be my motto in life and death. Amen.

V. In Honor of the Angels

Michael

14. Prayer to Saint Michael

St. Michael the Archangel, defend us in battle; be our defense against the wickedness and snares of the devil. May God rebuke him, we humbly pray. And do thou, O prince of the heavenly host, by the power of God thrust into hell Satan and all the evil spirits who prowl about the world for the ruin of souls. Amen.

15. O Most Glorious Prince
O most glorious Prince, Saint Michael the Archangel, I, thy most humble servant, salute thee through the most beloved Heart of Jesus Christ which I lovingly offer for the increase of thy joy and thy glory. I give thanks to God for the blessedness which He brings to thee and with which He wishes to honor and exalt thee above all the other Angels. I especially commend myself to thy care in life and death. Be with me now and always, especially at the end of my life. Kindly console me, strengthen me, and protect me. Obtain for me an increase in faith, hope, and charity. Do not permit me to stray from the holy faith, nor fall into the snare of desperation, nor to take for granted good works, which I am engaged in through the grace of God. Obtain for me pardon of my sins, humility, patience and the other virtues, true perseverance in goodness, and the final grace that I may give glory to God with thee forever. Amen.

Gabriel
16. O Strength of God
O strength of God, Saint Gabriel, thou who announced to the Virgin Mary the incarnation of the only-begotten Son of God, I praise thee and honor thee, O elect spirit. I humbly beg thee, with Jesus Christ our Savior and with His Blessed Mother, to be my advocate. I also pray that thou wouldst comfort me and strengthen me in all my difficulties, lest at any time I may be overcome by temptation and I might offend God by sinning. Amen.

17. Prayer to St. Gabriel, for Intercession
O Blessed Archangel Gabriel, we beseech thee, do thou intercede for us at the throne of divine Mercy in our present necessities, that as thou didst announce to Mary the mystery of the Incarnation, so through thy prayers and patronage in heaven we may obtain the benefits of the

same, and sing the praise of God forever in the land of the living. Amen.

18. Prayer to St. Gabriel, for Others
O loving messenger of the Incarnation, descend upon all those for whom I wish peace and happiness. Spread your wings over the cradles of the new-born babes, O thou who didst announce the coming of the Infant Jesus. Give to the young a lily petal from the virginal scepter in your hand. Cause the Ave Maria to re-echo in all hearts that they may find grace and joy through Mary. Finally, recall the sublime words spoken on the day of the Annunciation – "Nothing is impossible with God," and repeat them in hours of trial – to all I love – that their confidence in Our Lord may be reanimated, when all human help fails. Amen.

Raphael
19. O Heavenly Doctor
O heavenly doctor and most faithful companion, saint Raphael, thou who didst restore sight to the elder Tobit, and didst escort the younger Tobias throughout his appointed journey and kept him safe and sound, be the doctor of my body and soul. Dispel the darkness of my ignorance, and assist me in the dangerous journey of this life always, until thou leadeth me to my heavenly homeland. Amen.

20. Prayer to Saint Raphael, the Archangel
Glorious Archangel, Saint Raphael, great prince of the heavenly Court, you are illustrious for your gifts of wisdom and grace. You are a guide of those who journey by land, or sea, or air, consoler of the afflicted, and refuge of sinners. I beg you, assist me in all my needs and in all the sufferings of this life, as once you helped the young Tobias on his travels. Because you are the "medicine of God" I humbly pray you to heal the many infirmities of my soul and the ills that afflict my body. I especially ask of you the favor of

(here name your request) and the great grace of purity to prepare me to be the temple of the Holy Ghost. Amen.

21. Prayer to St. Raphael, Angel of Happy Meetings
O Raphael, lead us towards those we are waiting for, those who are waiting for us! Raphael, Angel of Happy Meetings, lead us by the hand towards those we are looking for! May all our movements, all their movements, be guided by your Light and transfigured by your Joy. Angel Guide of Tobias, lay the request we now address to you at the feet of Him on whose unveiled Face you are privileged to gaze. Lonely and tired, crushed by the separations and sorrows of earth, we feel the need of calling to you and of pleading for the protection of your wings, so that we may not be as strangers in the Province of Joy, all ignorant of the concerns of our country. Remember the weak, you who are strong--you whose home lies beyond the region of thunder, in a land that is always peaceful, always serene, and bright with the resplendent glory of God. Amen.

Guardian Angels
22. Angel of God (Guardian Angel Prayer)
Angel of God, my guardian dear,
To whom his love commits me here;
Ever this night be at my side,
To light and guard, to rule and guide. Amen.

23. Prayer to One's Guardian Angel
I believe that thou art the holy angel appointed by almighty God to watch over me. On this account, I beg and humbly implore thee, through Him who hast ordained thee to this task, that in this life thou wouldst always and everywhere guard me, wretched, weak, and unworthy that I am. Protect and defend me from all evil, and when God has bid my soul to leave this world, permit not the devil to have any power over it. Rather that thou wouldst gently take it from my

body and lead it sweetly unto the bosom of Abraham with the biding and assistance of God our Creator and Savior, who is blessed for ever. Amen.

24. Prayer before Starting on a Journey
My holy Angel Guardian, ask the Lord to bless the journey which I undertake, that it may profit the health of my soul and body; that I may reach its end, and that, returning safe and sound, I may find my family in good health. Do thou guard, guide and preserve us. Amen.

VI. In Honor of the Saints
25. St. Alphonsus De Liguori's Conclusion to a Short Treatise on Prayer
Let us pray, then, and let us always be asking for grace, if we wish to be saved. Let prayer be our most delightful occupation; let prayer be the exercise of our whole life. And when we are asking for particular graces, let us always pray for the grace to continue to pray for the future; because if we leave off praying we shall be lost. There is nothing easier than prayer. What does it cost us to say, Lord, stand by me! Lord, help me! Give me Thy love! And the like? What can be easier than this? But if we do not do so, we cannot be saved. Let us pray, then, and let us always shelter ourselves behind the intercession of Mary: "Let us seek for grace, and let us seek it through Mary," says St. Bernard. And when we recommend ourselves to Mary, let us be sure that she hears us and obtains for us whatever we want. She cannot lack either the power or the will to help us, as the same saint says: "Neither means nor will can be wanting to her." And St. Augustine addresses her: "Remember, O most pious Lady, that it has never been heard that any one who fled to thy protection was forsaken." Remember that the case has never occurred of a person having recourse to thee, and having been abandoned. Ah, no, says St. Bonaventure, he who invokes

Mary, finds salvation; and therefore he calls her "the salvation of those who invoke her." Let us, then, in our prayers always invoke Jesus and Mary; and let us never neglect to pray.

I have done. But before concluding, I cannot help saying how grieved I feel when I see that though the Holy Scriptures and the Fathers so often recommend the practice of prayer, yet so few other religious writers, or confessors, or preachers, ever speak of it; or if they do speak of it, just touch upon it in a cursory way, and leave it. But I, seeing the necessity of prayer, say, that the great lesson which all spiritual books should inculcate on their readers, all preachers on their hearers, and all confessors on their penitents, is this, to pray always; thus they should admonish them to pray; pray, and never give up praying. If you pray, you will be certainly saved; if you do not pray, you will be certainly damned.

St. Anne
26. To Saint Anne
Good St. Anne, you were especially favored by God to be the mother of the most holy Virgin Mary, the Mother of our Savior. By your power with your most pure daughter and with her divine Son, kindly obtain for us the grace and the favor we now seek. Please secure for us also forgiveness of our past sins, the strength to perform faithfully our daily duties and the help we need to persevere in the love of Jesus and Mary. Amen.

27. For the Sick
O Good Saint Anne, so justly called the Mother of the infirm, the health of those who suffer from disease, look kindly upon the sick person for whom I pray. Alleviate their sufferings, cause them to sanctify them by patience, and by complete submission to divine will. Finally deign to obtain health for them and with it the firm resolution to

honor Jesus, Mary and yourself by the faithful performance of their Christian duties. Amen.

St. Anthony
28. Unfailing Prayer to St. Anthony
"Blessed be God in His Angels and in His Saints"
O Holy St. Anthony, gentlest of Saints, your love for God and Charity for His creatures, made you worthy, when on earth, to possess miraculous powers. Encouraged by this thought, I implore you to obtain for me *(request)*. O gentle and loving St. Anthony, whose heart was ever full of human sympathy, whisper my petition into the ears of the sweet Infant Jesus, who loved to be folded in your arms; and the gratitude of my heart will ever be yours. Amen.

29. Saint Anthony of Padua
Holy Saint Anthony, gentle and powerful in your help, your love for God and charity for His creatures, made you worthy, when on earth, to possess miraculous powers. Miracles waited on your word, which you were always ready to request for those in trouble or anxiety. Encouraged by this thought, I implore you to obtain for me (request). The answer to my prayer may require a miracle. Even so, you are the Saint of miracles. Gentle and loving Saint Anthony, whose heart is ever full of human sympathy, take my petition to the Infant Savior for whom you have such a great love, and the gratitude of my heart will ever be yours. Amen.

30. Saint Anthony, Consoler of the Afflicted
Dear St. Anthony, comforting the sorrowful is a Christian duty and a work of mercy. By word, attitude, and deed I should try to brighten their days and make their burden easier to bear. St. Anthony, Consoler of the Afflicted, may I remember when helping someone in sorrow that I am

helping Christ Himself. Kindly mention my pressing needs to Him. *(Name your petitions)*.

31. Saint Anthony, Disperser of Devils
Dear St. Anthony, it is still as St. Peter said: The devil prowls about, lion-like, looking for someone to devour. I confess that I don't always resist him; I sometimes toy with temptation. St. Anthony, Disperser of Devils, remind me of my duty to avoid all occasions of sin. May I always pray in temptation that I may remain loyal to my Lord Jesus. Pray for my other intentions, please. *(Name them.)*

32. Saint Anthony, Example of Humility
Dear St. Anthony, after all these years in the school of Christ, I still haven't learned the lesson of true humility. My feelings are easily ruffled. Quick to take offense, I am slow to forgive. St. Anthony, Example of Humility, teach me the importance and necessity of this Christian virtue. In the presence of Jesus, who humbled Himself and whom the Father exalted, remember also these special intentions of mine. *(Name them.)*

33. Saint Anthony, Generator of Charity
Dear St. Anthony, God wants us to see Christ, our brother, in everyone and love Him truly in word and in deed. God wills that we share with others the joy of His boundless love. St. Anthony, Generator of Charity, remember me in the Father's presence, that I may be generous in sharing the joy of His love. Remember also the special intentions I now entrust to you. *(Name them.)*

34. Saint Anthony, Guide of Pilgrims
Dear St. Anthony, we are all pilgrims. We came from God and we are going to Him. He who created us will welcome us at journey's end. The Lord Jesus is preparing a place for all His brothers and sisters. St. Anthony, Guide of Pilgrims,

direct my steps in the straight path. Protect me until I am safely home in heaven. Help me in all my needs and difficulties. (*Name them.*)

35. Saint Anthony, Liberator of Prisoners

Dear St. Anthony, I am imprisoned by walls of selfishness, prejudice, suspicion. I am enslaved by human respect and the fear of other people's opinions of me. St. Anthony, Liberator of Prisoners, tear down my prison walls. Break the chains that hold me captive. Make me free with the freedom Christ has won for me. To your powerful intercession I also recommend these intentions. (*Name them.*)

36. Saint Anthony, Martyr of Desire

Dear St. Anthony, you became a Franciscan with the hope of shedding your blood for Christ. In God's plan for you, your thirst for martyrdom was never to be satisfied. St. Anthony, Martyr of Desire, pray that I may become less afraid to stand up and be counted as a follower of the Lord Jesus. Intercede also for my other intentions. (*Name them.*)

37. Saint Anthony, Model of Perfection

Dear St. Anthony, you took the words of Jesus seriously, "Be perfect, even as your heavenly Father is perfect." The Church honors you as a Christian hero, a man wholly dedicated to God's glory and the good of the redeemed. St. Anthony, Model of Perfection, ask Jesus to strengthen my good dispositions and to make me more like you, more like Him. Obtain for me the other favors I need. (*Name them.*)

38. Saint Anthony, Performer of Miracles

Dear St. Anthony, your prayers obtained miracles during your lifetime. You still seem to move at ease in the realm of minor and major miracles. St. Anthony, Performer of Miracles, please obtain for me the blessings God holds in reserve who serve Him. Pray that I may be worthy of the promises my Lord Jesus attaches to confident prayer. (*Mention your special intentions.*)

39. Saint Anthony, Restorer of Sight to the Blind
Dear St. Anthony, you recall the Gospel episode about the blind man who, partly healed, could see men "looking like walking trees." After a second laying-on of Jesus's hands, he could see perfectly. St. Anthony, Restorer of Sight to the Blind, please sharpen my spiritual vision. May I see people, not as trees or numbers, but as sons and daughters of the Most High. Help me in my pressing needs. (*Name your special intentions.*)

40. Saint Anthony, Restorer of Speech to the Mute
Dear St. Anthony, how tongue-tied I can be when I should be praising God and defending the oppressed. My cowardice often strikes me dumb; I am afraid to open my mouth. St. Anthony, Restorer of Speech to the Mute, release me from my fears. Teach me to praise God and to champion the rights of those unjustly treated. Please remember also all my intentions. (*Name them.*)

41. Saint Anthony, Zealous for Justice
Dear St. Anthony, you were prompt to fulfill all justice. You gave God and His creation the service He required from you. You respected other people's rights and treated them with kindness and understanding. St. Anthony, Zealous for Justice, teach me the beauty of this virtue. Make me prompt to fulfill all justice toward God and toward all creation. Help me also in my pressing needs. (*Name them.*)

St. Blase
42. O glorious Saint Blase, who by thy martyrdom has left to the Church a precious witness to the faith, obtain for us

the grace to preserve within ourselves this divine gift, and to defend, without human respect, both by word and example, the truth of that same faith, which is so wickedly attacked and slandered in these our times. Thou who didst miraculously cure a little child when it was at the point of death by reason of an affliction of the throat, grant us thy powerful protection in like misfortunes; and, above all, obtain for us the grace of Christian mortification together with a faithful observance of the precepts of the Church, which may keep us from offending Almighty God. Amen.

St. Christopher
43. St. Chistopher, patron of travellers, to you I entrust myself and those who will accompany me on my journey, praying you to keep us from all harm and to bring us safely to our destination. O great saint, true Christ-bearer, who converted multitudes to the Christian faith and who for love of Jesus Christ suffered cruel torments in your martyrdom, I implore your intercession to enable me to avoid every sin, the only real evil. Preserve me and those dear to me against the forces of the elements, such as earthquakes, tornadoes, lightning, fire and flood, and guide us safely through the dangers of this life to the eternal shores. Amen.

44. Patron of Motorists
Dear Saint, you have inherited a beautiful name – Christopher – as a result of a wonderful legend that while carrying people across a raging stream you also carried the Child Jesus. Teach us to be true "Christ-bearers" to those who do not know Him. Protect all drivers who often transport those who bear Christ within them. Amen.

St. Dymphna
45. Prayer to St. Dymphna – Charity
You are celebrated St. Dymphna, for your goodness to others. Both in your lifetime, and even more in the ages

since, you have again and again demonstrated your concern for those who are mentally disturbed or emotionally troubled. Kindly secure for me, then, some measure of your own serene love, and ask our Lord to give us a share in His life and boundless charity. Amen.

46. Prayer to St. Dymphna – Chastity
Most pure virgin, St. Dymphna, we live at a time when many are intent on satisfying every carnal appetite. Your single-minded dedication to Christ alone is providential and inspiring. Please help us by your power with God to see life in proportion as you did. With your aid we propose to perform all our actions for a pure motive, and promptly to resist all our evil inclinations. Amen.

47. Prayer to St. Dymphna – Faith
Dear St. Dymphna, you gave us an example in your own life of firm faith. Neither flattery, earthly rewards nor the threat of death caused you to waver in your fidelity to God. Please help us then, amid the uncertainties of life, to imitate your wholehearted dedication to Christ. Be good enough to come to our aid in our need, and pray for us to God. Amen.

48. Prayer to St. Dymphna – Fortitude
Courageous St. Dymphna, your strength was from God. His grace enabled you to resist evil, and to prefer exile to a life of sinful luxury. Christ's own power preserved you faithful to Him in life and in death. In your kindness help us to imitate your example in little things, and gain for us fortitude to bear with the misfortunes we meet, and strength to overcome our weakness. Amen.

49. Prayer to St. Dymphna – Hope
Good St. Dymphna, you placed all your hope in Christ's promises, and sacrificed even your life in that hope. The Lord, God, rewarded your constancy by making your name

known and loved over many centuries by the thousands whom you have aided in time of difficulty. Please assist us now in our present necessity, and intercede before God for our intentions. Obtain for us a firm hope like your own in God's unfailing protection. Amen.

50. Prayer to St. Dymphna – Justice
Admirable St. Dymphna, how just you were to all whom you encountered, and how careful you were to give every person his due, and more than he might desire or expect. By your power with God please come to assist us to be just to all we meet, and even to be generous in giving everyone more than strict justice requires. Amen.

51. Prayer to St. Dymphna – Perseverance
Most faithful St. Dymphna, you remained true to your baptismal promises to the very end. You are, therefore, honored, known, and loved after 1,400 years by people you have aided all over the world. We do not know how long or short a time is left to us of this life here, but help us in any case to be faithful to God to the end. Please gain for us the grace to live one day at a time as if each were to be our last. Amen.

52. Prayer to St. Dymphna – Prudence
You were marked in life, St. Dymphna, by a high degree of prudence. You sought and followed the advice of your confessor and spiritual guide. You fled from temptation even when it meant exile and poverty. In your last extremity you chose to die rather than offend God. Please help us now by your merits not only to know what is right, but procure for us also the strength to do it. Amen.

53. Prayer to St. Dymphna – Temperance
Generous St. Dymphna, like all Christ's martyrs you gained this crowning grace because you prepared for it by a life of

self denial. By faithfulness in smaller things you were ready for your final trial. Please teach us by your example and help to use the good things of life so that we may not miss our chance for life eternal. Help us, too, to watch and pray for ourselves and others. Amen.

54. Saint Dymphna
Lord, our God, you graciously chose St. Dymphna as patroness of those afflicted with mental and nervous disorders. She is thus an inspiration and a symbol of charity to the thousands who ask her intercession. Please grant, Lord, through the prayers of this pure youthful martyr, relief and consolation to all suffering such trials, and especially those for whom we pray. (*Here mention those for whom you wish to pray*). We beg you, Lord, to hear the prayers of St. Dymphna on our behalf. Grant all those for whom we pray patience in their sufferings and resignation to your divine will. Please fill them with hope, and grant them the relief and cure they so much desire. We ask this through Christ our Lord who suffered agony in the garden. Amen.

St. Francis of Assisi
55. Dear Saint, once worldly and vain, you became humble and poor for the sake of Jesus and had extraordinary love for the Crucified, which showed itself in your body by the stigmata, the imprints of Christ's Sacred Wounds. In our selfish and sensual age, how greatly we need your secret that draws countless men and women to imitate you. Teach us also great love for the poor and unswerving loyalty to the Vicar of Christ, our Holy Father the Pope. Amen.

St. Francis Xavier Cabrini
56. Great St. Francis, well beloved and full of charity, in union with you I reverently adore the Divine Majesty, and since I specially rejoice in the singular gifts of grace

bestowed on you in life and of glory after death, I give thanks to God, and beg of you, with all the affection of my heart, that by your powerful intercession you may obtain for me above all things the grace to live a holy life and die a holy death. Moreover, I beg of you to obtain for me (*here mention special spiritual or temporal favor*); but if what I ask does not tend to the glory of God and the greater good of my soul, do you, I beseech you, obtain for me what will more certainly attain these ends. Amen.
(Our Father, Hail Mary, Glory Be).

St. Gerard Majella
57. For Motherhood
Good St. Gerard, powerful intercessor before the throne of God, wonder-worker of our day, I call upon you and seek your aid. You know that my husband and I desire the gift of a child. Please present our fervent plea to the Creator of life from whom all parenthood proceeds and beseech him to bless us with a child whom we may raise as his child and heir of heaven. Amen.

58. In thanks for a Safe Delivery
Good St. Gerard, patron of mothers, assist me in thanking God for the great gift of motherhood. During the months of my waiting, I learned to call upon you and placed the safety of my child and myself under your powerful protection. The great lesson of your trust in God sustained me; your slogan, "God will provide," became my hope and consolation. I thank God for a healthy and normal baby and my own good health. Help me to prize the great treasure of motherhood and obtain for me the grace to raise my child as a child of God. In gratitude, I will continue to call upon you and will tell other mothers about their special patron and friend. Amen.

59. For Special Intentions

Almighty and loving Father, I thank you for giving St. Gerard to us as a most appealing model and powerful friend. By his example, he showed us how to love and trust you. You have showered many blessings on those who call upon him. For your greater glory and my welfare, please grant me the favors which I ask in his name. (*Here mention them privately*) And you, my powerful patron, intercede for me before the throne of God. Draw near to that throne and do not leave it until you have been heard. O good saint, to you I address my fervent prayers; graciously accept them and let me experience in some way the effects of your powerful intercession. Amen.

60. Prayer of the Expectant Mother to Saint Gerard Majella

O Great Saint Gerard, beloved servant of Jesus Christ, perfect imitator of thy meek and humble Savior, and devoted Child of the Mother of God: enkindle within my heart one spark of that heavenly fire of charity which glowed in thine and made thee a seraph of love. O glorious Saint Gerard, because when falsely accused of crime, thou didst bear, like thy Divine Master, without murmur or complaint, the calumnies of wicked men, thou hast been raised up by God as Patron and Protector of expectant mothers. Preserve me from danger and from excessive pains accompanying childbirth, and shield the child which I now carry, that he or she may see the light of day and receive the lustral waters of baptism, through Jesus Christ our Lord. (*say nine Hail Mary's, one for each month of pregnancy*).

61. For a Sick Child

St. Gerard, who, like the Savior, loved children so tenderly and by your prayers freed many from disease and even death, listen to us who are pleading for our sick child. We thank God for the great gift of our son (daughter) and ask him to restore our child to health if such be his holy will. This favor, we beg of you through your love for all children and mothers. Amen.

St. John Bosco

62. O glorious Saint John Bosco, who in order to lead young people to the feet of the divine Master and to mould them in the light of faith and Christian morality didst heroically sacrifice thyself to the very end of thy life and didst set up a proper religious Institute destined to endure and to bring to the farthest boundaries of the earth thy glorious work, obtain also for us from Our Lord a holy love for young people who are exposed to so many seductions in order that we may generously spend ourselves in supporting them against the snares of the devil, in keeping them safe from the dangers of the world, and in guiding them, pure and holy, in the path that leads to God. Amen.

St. Jude

63. Prayer to Saint Jude - Patron of Desperate Causes
Saint Jude, apostle of Christ, the Church honors and prays to you universally as the patron of hopeless and difficult cases. Pray for us in our needs. Make use, we implore you, of this powerful privilege given to you to bring visible and speedy help where help is needed. Pray that we humbly accept trials and disappointments and mistakes which are apart of human nature. Let us see the reflection of the sufferings of Christ in our daily trials and tribulations. Let us see in a spirit of great faith and hope the part we even now share in the joy of Christ's resurrection, and which we long to share fully in heaven. Intercede that we may again experience this joy in answer to our present needs if it is God's Will. *(Make request here...)* Amen

64. Most holy Apostle St. Jude, faithful servant and friend of Jesus, the name of the traitor who delivered the beloved

Master into the hands of His enemies has caused you to be forgotten by many, but the Church honors and invokes you universally as the patron of hopeless cases, of things despaired of. Pray for me who am so miserable; make use, I implore you, of this particular privilege accorded to you, to bring visible and speedy help, where help is almost despaired of. Come to my assistance in this great need, that I may receive the consolations and succor of Heaven in all my necessities, tribulations and sufferings, particularly (*here make your request*), and that I may bless God with you and all the elect forever. I promise you, O blessed St. Jude, to be ever mindful of this great favor, and I will never cease to honor you as my special and powerful patron and to do all in my power to encourage devotion to you. Amen.

65. St. Jude, glorious Apostle, faithful servant and friend of Jesus, the name of the traitor has caused you to be forgotten by many, but the true Church invokes you universally as the Patron of things despaired of; pray for me, that finally I may receive the consolations and the succor of Heaven in all my necessities, tribulations, and sufferings, particularly (here make your request), and that I may bless God with the Elect throughout Eternity. Amen.

St. Lucy
66. Saint Lucy, whose beautiful name signifies light, by the light of Faith which God bestowed upon you, increase and preserve his light in my soul, so that I may avoid evil, be zealous in the performance of good works, and abhor nothing so much as the blindness and the darkness of evil and sin. Obtain for me, by your intercession with God, perfect vision for my bodily eyes and the grace to use them for God's greater honor and glory and the salvation of souls. St. Lucy, virgin and martyr, hear my prayers and obtain my petitions. Amen.

St. Martin de Porres
67. To you Saint Martin de Porres we prayerfully lift up our hearts filled with serene confidence and devotion. Mindful of your unbounded and helpful charity to all levels of society and also of your meekness and humility of heart, we offer our petitions to you. Pour out upon our families the precious gifts of your solicitous and generous intercession; show to the people of every race and every color the paths of unity and of justice; implore from our Father in heaven the coming of his kingdom, so that through mutual benevolence in God men may increase the fruits of grace and merit the rewards of eternal life. Amen.

St. Monica
68. Prayer to St. Monica - Patroness of Mothers Exemplary
Mother of the great Augustine, for 30 years you perseveringly pursued your wayward son with love and affection and pardon and counsel and powerful cries to Heaven. Intercede for all mothers in our day so that they may learn to draw their children to God and to His Holy Church. Teach them how to remain close to their children, even the prodigal sons and daughters who have sadly gone so far astray. Amen.

St. Patrick
69. Lorica of Saint Patrick (By St. Patrick, c.a. 377)
I arise today
Through a mighty strength, the invocation of the Trinity,
Through a belief in the Threeness,
Through confession of the Oneness
Of the Creator of creation.

I arise today
Through the strength of Christ's birth and His baptism,
Through the strength of His crucifixion and His burial,
Through the strength of His resurrection and His ascension,

Through the strength of His descent for the judgment of doom.

I arise today
Through the strength of the love of cherubim,
In obedience of angels,
In service of archangels,
In the hope of resurrection to meet with reward,
In the prayers of patriarchs,
In preachings of the apostles,
In faiths of confessors,
In innocence of virgins,
In deeds of righteous men.

I arise today
Through the strength of heaven;
Light of the sun,
Splendor of fire,
Speed of lightning,
Swiftness of the wind,
Depth of the sea,
Stability of the earth,
Firmness of the rock.

I arise today
Through God's strength to pilot me;
God's might to uphold me,
God's wisdom to guide me,
God's eye to look before me,
God's ear to hear me,
God's word to speak for me,
God's hand to guard me,
God's way to lie before me,
God's shield to protect me,
God's hosts to save me

From snares of the devil,
From temptations of vices,
From every one who desires me ill,
Afar and anear,
Alone or in a mulitude.

I summon today all these powers between me and evil,
Against every cruel merciless power that opposes my body and soul,
Against incantations of false prophets,
Against black laws of pagandom,
Against false laws of heretics,
Against craft of idolatry,
Against spells of women and smiths and wizards,
Against every knowledge that corrupts man's body and soul.
Christ shield me today
Against poison, against burning,
Against drowning, against wounding,
So that reward may come to me in abundance.

Christ with me,
Christ before me,
Christ behind me,
Christ in me,
Christ beneath me,
Christ above me,
 Christ on my right,
Christ on my left,
Christ when I lie down,
Christ when I sit down,
Christ in the heart of every man who thinks of me,
Christ in the mouth of every man who speaks of me,
Christ in the eye that sees me,
Christ in the ear that hears me.

I arise today
Through a mighty strength, the invocation of the Trinity,
Through a belief in the Threeness,
Through a confession of the Oneness
Of the Creator of creation

St. Peregrine, the "Cancer Saint"
70. Glorious Wonder-Worker, St. Peregrine, you answered the divine call, with a ready spirit, and forsook all the comforts of the world to dedicate yourself to God in the Order of His most Holy Mother. You labored manfully for the salvation of souls; and in union with Jesus Crucified you endured the most painful sufferings with such patience as to deserve to be healed miraculously of an incurable cancer-in your leg by a touch of His divine hand. Obtain for me the grace to answer every call of God and to fulfill His will in all the events of life. Enkindle in my heart a consuming zeal for the salvation of souls; deliver me from the infirmities that afflict my body (*especially...*). Obtain for me also perfect resignation to the sufferings it may please God to send me, so that, imitating our Crucified Savior and His Sorrowful Mother, I may merit eternal glory in heaven. Amen.
St. Peregrine, pray for me and for all who invoke your aid. *(3 times).*

St. Peter
71. O glorious Saint Peter, who, in return for thy strong and generous faith, thy profound and sincere humility, and they burning love, wast rewarded by Jesus Christ with singular privileges, and, in particular, with the leadership of the other Apostles and the primacy of the whole Church, of which thou wast made the foundation stone, do thou obtain for us the grace of a lively faith, that shall not fear to profess itself openly, in its entirety and in all of its manifestations, even to the shedding of blood, if occasion

should demand it, and to sacrifice of life itself rather than surrender. Obtain for us likewise, a sincere loyalty to our holy mother, the Church; grant that we may ever remain most closely and sincerely united to the Roman Pontiff, who is the heir of thy faith and of thy authority, the one, true, visible Head of the Catholic Church, that mystic ark outside of which there is no salvation. Grant, moreover, that we may follow, in all humility and meekness, her teaching and her advice, and may be obedient to all her precepts, in order to be able here on earth to enjoy a peace that is sure and undisturbed, and to attain one day in heaven to everlasting happiness. Amen.

V. Pray for us, Saint Peter the Apostle,
R. That we may be made worthy of the promises of Christ.

Let us pray.
O God, who hast given unto Thy blessed Apostle Peter the keys to the kingdom of heaven, and the power to bind and loose: grant that we may be delivered, through the help of this intercession, from the slavery of all our sins: Who livest and reignest world without end. Amen.

St. Pius X
72. Glorious Pope of the Eucharist, St. Pius X, who sought to restore all things in Christ, obtain for me a true love of Jesus that I may live only for Him. Help me, that, with lively fervor and a sincere will to strive for sanctity of life, I may daily avail myself of the riches of the Holy Eucharist in Sacrifice and Sacrament. By your love for Mary Mother and Queen of all, inflame my heart with tender devotion to her. Blessed model of the priesthood, obtain for us holy and zealous priests and increase vocations to the religious life. Dispel heresy and incline hearts to peace and concord, that all nations may place themselves under the sweet reign of Christ. Amen.

St. Pius X, pray for me, that (*mention any particular intention*).

Prayer to St Rita - Patroness of Impossible Cases
73. Holy Patroness of those in need, Saint Rita, your pleadings before your divine Lord are irresistible. For your lavishness in granting favors you have been called the "Advocate of the Hopeless" and even of the "Impossible." You are so humble, so mortified, so patient, so compassionate in love for your crucified Jesus that you can obtain from Him anything you ask if it is His Holy Will. Therefore, all confidently have recourse to you in hope of comfort or relief. Be propitious toward your suppliants and show your power with God in their behalf. Be generous with your favors now as you have been in so many wonderful cases for the greater glory of God, the spread of your devotion, and the consolation of those who trust in you. We promise, if our petition be granted, to glorify you by making known your favor, and to bless you and sing your praises. Relying then on your merits and power before the Sacred Heart of Jesus, we ask you (*Name your request*). Amen.

St. Teresa of Avila
74. O Saint Teresa, seraphic Virgin, beloved spouse of thy crucified Lord, thou who on earth didst burn with a love so intense toward thy God and my God, and now dost glow with a brighter and purer flame in paradise: obtain for me also, I beseech thee, a spark of that same holy fire which shall cause me to forget the world, all things created, and even myself; for thou didst ever avidly desire to see Him loved by all men. Grant that my every thought and desire and affection may be continually directed to doing the will of God, the supreme Good, whether I am in joy or in pain, for He is worthy to be loved and obeyed forever. Obtain for

me this grace, thou who art so powerful with God; may I be all on fire, like thee, with the holy love of God. Amen.

St. Therese of Lisieux
75. I greet you, Saint Therese of the Child Jesus, lily of purity, ornament and glory of Christianity! I salute you, great saint, seraph of Divine Love. I rejoice at the favors our Blessed Lord Jesus has liberally bestowed on you. In humility and confidence I entreat you to help me, for 1 know that God has given you charity and pity as well as power. Oh then, behold my distress, my anxiety, my fears. Oh, tell Him now my wants. One sigh from you will crown my success, will fill me with joy. Remember your promise to do good on earth. Obtain for me from God the graces of our Divine Lord, especially (*Name your request*). Amen.

76. O wondrous Saint Theresa of the Child Jesus, who, in thy brief earthly life, didst become a mirror of angelic purity, of courageous love and of whole-hearted surrender to Almighty God, now that thou art enjoying the reward of thy virtues, turn thine eyes of mercy upon us who trust in thee. Obtain for us the grace to keep our hearts and minds pure and clean like unto thine, and to detest in all sincerity whatever might tarnish ever so slightly the luster of a virtue so sublime, a virtue that endears us to they heavenly Bridegroom. Ah, dear Saint, grant us to feel in every need the power of thy intercession; give us comfort in all the bitterness of this life and especially at its latter end, that we may be worthy to share eternal happiness with thee in paradise. Amen.

V. Pray for us, O blessed Theresa,
R. That we may be made worthy of the promises of Christ.

Let us pray.

O Lord, who has said: "Unless you become as little children, you shall not enter into the kingdom of heaven;" grant us, we beseech Thee, so to walk in the footsteps of thy blessed Virgin Theresa with a humble and single heart, that we may attain to everlasting rewards: Who livest and reignest world without end. Amen.

Prayer to One's Patron or Any Saint
77. O Glorious Saint N. (*my beloved Patron*), you served God in humility and confidence on earth and are now in the enjoyment of His beatific Vision in heaven because you persevered till death and gained the crown of eternal life. Remember now the dangers that surround me in the vale of tears, and intercede for me in my needs and troubles (*Name your request*)

To the Holy Souls in Purgatory
78. O Holy Souls in Purgatory, who are the certain heirs of heaven, souls most dear to Jesus as the trophies of His Precious Blood and to Mary, Mother of Mercy, obtain for me through your intercession the grace to lead a holy life, to die a happy death and to attain to the blessedness of eternity in heaven. Dear Suffering Souls, who languish in your prison of pain and long to be delivered in order to praise and glorify God in heaven, by your unfailing pity help me at this time, particularly (*Name your request*), that I may obtain relief and assistance from God. In gratitude for your intercession I offer to God on your behalf the satisfactory merits of all my works and sufferings of this day (*week, month, or whatever space of time you wish to designate.*)

APPENDIX B. OILS AND INCENSES

(This appendix is also not found in the Kindle edition)

This list is far from exhaustive, and intended to give a starting point that you'll expand as you grow in your Candle Magic practices. As you move forward in experience, you'll find that some of these works for you and some don't, and you'll find others that work even better. Feel free to make note of when this happens and incorporate the new information into your personal practice.

These items may be used either as essential oils or as incense in stick, cone, or resin form.

Blessing: acacia, angelica, carnation, frankincense, jasmine, lavender, lily of the valley, lotus.

Banishing: cedar, sage, sweetgrass, frankincense and myrrh, rosemary.

Creativity: honeysuckle, lilac, lotus, rose, cherry, savory.

Energy or Power: allspice, bay, cinnamon, frankincense, lotus, musk, thyme, dragon's blood.

Good luck: cedar, mint, violet, nutmeg, bayberry, cinnamon, jasmine.

Harmony: apple blossom, basil, cedar, lavender, lilac, orange, rose, lily of the valley.

Healing: carnation, cinnamon, clove, lavender, lotus, myrrh, rose.

Inspiration: acacia, clove, laurel, lily of the valley.

Love: apple blossom, civit, gardenia, honeysuckle, jasmine, musk, rose.

Meditation: angelica, frankincense and myrrh.

Protection: angelica, bay, dragon's blood, frankincense and myrrh, lily of the valley.

Psychic Development: frankincense, sandalwood.

Willpower: cinnamon, dragon's blood, st. johnswort.

NOTES:

NOTES:

NOTES:

NOTES:

Made in the USA
Las Vegas, NV
04 March 2022